Spanish Beef and Rice, page 107

BEST OF THE BEST
Presents

Favorite Slow Cooker Recipes

Bob Warden

with Christian Stella

QUAIL RIDGE PRESS
Preserving America's Food Heritage

Published by Quail Ridge Press and Great Chefs International

First printing, March 2013 • Second, March 2013 • Third, June 2013 • Fourth, March 2014
Fifth, October 2014

Author photograph ©Benoit Cortet

Book Design and Food Photography by
Christian and Elise Stella

On the front cover: Pork Cassoulet, page 147

On the back cover: Slow Cooker Pot Roast, page 87 • All Day Chili, page 39
Slow Cooker Mac and Cheese, page 71 • Chicken and Biscuit Pot Pie, page 113

ISBN 978-1-934193-88-4
Library of Congress Control Number: 2013930152

Manufactured in the United States of America

QUAIL RIDGE PRESS
www.quailridge.com

Contents

Introduction

I set out to write this book after seeing that modern slow cooker books were getting farther and farther away from what the slow cooker is truly good at—cooking low and slow, melt-in-your-mouth meals without standing all day over a hot stove. Slow cooking is all about convenience: the convenience of cooking a meal for the entire family in one pot, and the convenience of letting it cook as you go about the rest of your day. That was my goal for the recipes in this book, for the majority of them to be as convenient as they are delicious.

I am most known for working with pressure cookers and have sold over 250,000 copies of my cookbooks on pressure cooking. Writing a book on slow cooking would seem to be the exact opposite of my expertise, but slow cooking shares nearly everything in common with pressure cooking, other than the cook times! One might ask why anyone would bother slow cooking when pressure cooking can get the job done so much quicker, but I understand that the true value to slow cooking is having a home-cooked meal ready whenever you are. It's all about that moment you walk in the door from a day out and smell dinner, which has (seemingly) cooked itself while you were gone. And it's all about having recipes that allow you the freedom to leave them be, without a worry in the world.

It is for this reason that I have tried to make most of the recipes in this book take as long to cook as possible, the exact opposite of my previous books. The perfect slow cooker recipe is one that you can quickly prep before work, and one that takes your entire work day to cook. The perfect slow cooker recipe is one that can withstand going over the recommended cook time if you are late to get home. And the perfect slow cooker recipe is one that can please the whole family.

Nearly all slow cooker recipes today are made with canned soups and other packaged ingredients. While this is very simple, it doesn't always make for the best tasting dish, and it certainly doesn't give you that warm and fuzzy feeling you get from making something from scratch. I have done my best to avoid the use of canned or packaged ingredients while still keeping my recipes simple and *convenient*. There are hundreds of books out there that tell you how to cook a cut of meat in canned soup, but there are surprisingly few that will tell you how to cook that same type of dish from scratch. I can only hope that you enjoy my approach to slow cooking as much as I do. There is always a bit of magic when you toss a few ingredients into a slow cooker and dinner comes out, but there is even more magic when the ingredients are simpler, fresher, and better tasting.

These are my favorite slow cooker recipes. Some were reinvented from all-time classics, and some reinvented using fresher ingredients, some simply staples in my household, and some are entirely new ideas that push the slow cooker into the modern era. As our lives get ever more complicated and we get ever busier, slow cooking can ensure that we all have dinner ready the instant we come home . . . that we can all create a little magic.

Round or Oval Cookers

All recipes in this book are suitable for a four-quart slow cooker or larger, unless otherwise noted. The dip recipes in this book can be made in smaller, dip-sized cookers as well—but that is not necessary. Recipes should work in your cooker whether it is round or oval. The only benefit to using an oval cooker for these recipes is that it will be easier to cut and serve casserole dishes, and easier to fit larger cuts of meat. If a cut of meat does not fit into your round cooker, simply cut it in half.

About Cooking Times

Cooking times in this book were tested in at least two different models of slow cookers. That said, there is no set standard operating temperature for slow cookers, and many models and brands can differ by several degrees. While only a few degrees might not sound like much, over several hours, the difference can add up. I have tried my best to adapt my recipes to stand up to these variations in temperature, but it is recommended that (until you are fully familiar with your cooker) you check for doneness early in recipes that are dense or contain dairy, as a slow cooker that runs several degrees higher than others may scorch them. In general, most modern slow cookers cook at a higher temperature than vintage models. Though I consider all slow cookers safe, many companies have raised their temperatures in the last decade to prevent any chance of food not reaching the proper temperature to kill bacteria. Because of this, recipes in this book with cook times under four hours may need additional time in older slow cookers.

As it should always be in the kitchen, let yourself be the best judge of when something is "done" to your liking.

The Best Kept Slow Cooker Secret

Few people know that slow cooking on LOW or HIGH is less about temperature and more about the time it takes for the food to reach the optimum temperature. Oftentimes there is no difference between cooking on LOW or HIGH other than how long the food will take to cook. As a general rule, cooking on LOW takes twice as long as cooking on HIGH. For this reason, most recipes in this book that are cooked on LOW can be cooked in exactly half of the time if cooked on HIGH. Most meat recipes can be cooked to tender in eight hours on LOW or four hours on HIGH.

Although this rule is pretty universal, I do not recommend converting the recipes in this book that are cooked on HIGH down to the LOW temperature by doubling the cook time. This can usually be done with slow cooker recipes, but I have limited the HIGH cooking recipes in this book to only ones that truly need to be cooked on HIGH, as I feel that most people want their slow cooker to cook slow, allowing them to prep their meals early in the day.

This is the reason that there are so few recipes in this book that cook on the HIGH temperature. All LOW recipes can be converted to HIGH by halving the cook time, but all HIGH recipes are best left to always cook on HIGH or they may not thicken or set properly.

General Slow Cooking Tips

- Unless otherwise mentioned in the recipe, using frozen meats is not recommended, and can add several hours to the cooking time, which will most likely overcook other ingredients in the dish. The same can be said about using frozen vegetables, though many recipes in this book do use frozen vegetables and have been optimized for the additional cook time.

- I encourage checking on recipes until you are comfortable with the cooking temperature and speed of your slow cooker, but it is also important to note that lifting the lid of your slow cooker will let heat escape and could add as much as 15 minutes to the cook time each time you do it. When checking on food, make it quick and infrequent to let the least amount of heat escape.

- Removing all chicken skin, and trimming meat of excess fat is recommended. As slow cooking heats in a moist environment, chicken skin will never crisp up, and fat won't always reach a high enough temperature to render (or melt) down. Trimming the excess fat is also better for your waistline! If you are a fan of crispy chicken skin though, may I suggest removing the skin and crisping it in a skillet, as you would cook bacon, to serve as a garnish alongside the finished dish? It's not just delicious, but often cooked this way in fine restaurants, as it ensures perfectly crisp skin.

- Watch for meat that contains an excessive amount of an added water solution. In recent years, meat processors have been adding a "flavoring" or "tenderizing" solution to meat. This solution is simply flavored and salted water that not only adds weight to the meat (that you pay for by the pound) but sodium as well. When slow cooking, the meat will release all of this added water and dilute the sauce it is cooking in. Read packages carefully to ensure that you are buying meat with the least amount of water added to ensure that you not only get what you are paying for, but get the best results from the recipes you are preparing. In general, all chicken has about 4% water added, and the recipes in this book reflect that. Pork can vary greatly with anywhere from no water added to 20% water added. Beef is just starting to show up on the shelves with water added but is still easy to avoid (and you should!). In general, meat with water added is usually vacuum sealed or packaged by a big name brand. Meat that is packaged on site by your grocer is usually the best bet. Thankfully, it is required by law to disclose the percentage of water solution added to meat.

- Cut ingredients into equal-sized pieces to ensure even cooking. This is especially true with potatoes and vegetables, as you don't want half of your potatoes to turn to mush before the other half are tender.

- Some of the recipes in this book call for whisking flour into the cooking liquid to thicken it. These recipes will turn out smoother if the liquid and flour are brought to a simmer over a stove (as you whisk) before adding to the slow cooker, though this is not necessary. For a perfectly smooth sauce (with no lumps) every time, replace flour with ¾ the amount of cornstarch. I prefer flour in the recipes I've used it in because flour and cornstarch lend different textures to the sauce, each having their own place. In general, flour is velvety but sometimes lumpy, while cornstarch makes for a perfectly smooth but slightly sticky sauce.

- I prefer to use evaporated milk in place of other types of dairy in most of my recipes because it is not only pantry-friendly, but holds up very well to cooking, with very little chance of curdling. That said, 1½ cups of whole milk can be substituted for evaporated milk in any recipe.

Using Beef and Chicken Bases

One of the principals of good cooking, especially slow cooking, is that you should never miss an opportunity to add flavor. It is for this reason that you may notice that nearly all of the recipes in this book use stocks or broths in place of water. Creating your own stock, while delicious, can be quite time consuming, and purchasing cans or cartons of pre-made stock or broth can get very expensive (and heavy). This is where bases come in.

I highly suggest purchasing beef and chicken bases to prepare the recipes in this book. A highly concentrated liquid or paste, these bases can be diluted (according to the jar or bottle's directions) to create instant stocks. While these bases may seem expensive at first, compare the cups of stock they will create with the costs of purchasing regular stock or broth, and you will find that you are saving quite a lot of money in the end.

Additionally, these bases tend to be far, far lower in sodium than other, less natural options like bouillon cubes. The other advantage of bases is that you can add more base to taste for even more robust sauces that taste like they've been reducing on the stove all day long. While none of the recipes in this book require you to add any extra base than

the package's recommended ratio, many of the gravies in these recipes will taste even better if you add an extra teaspoon or so to taste before serving.

Special Diets

This book is not a diet book, but I understand that many people have dietary restrictions that may limit their enjoyment of my recipes. It is difficult to create a cookbook that can please everyone and every dietary restriction. If you have a dietary restriction, please use your knowledge of that restriction to make substitutions that are better for your way of eating. While I understand that many people would like to see nutritional information included in this book, that information would not reflect the following changes that I suggest you make if you are on a restricted diet.

- For those that are on a reduced-sodium diet, it is recommended that you use low-sodium versions of stocks/broths, and reduce, omit, or replace any added salt in the recipe with a salt substitute.

- For those that are watching calories or fat, you can substitute leaner cuts of meat and trim any excess fat. You can also substitute low-fat dairy for the regular dairy products used in the recipes, and reduce or use nonstick cooking spray in place of oil. A light heart-healthy margarine such as Smart Balance® can be used in place of butter.

- For those with gluten intolerances, all flour used to dredge meat before browning can be omitted. Any sauce thickened with flour can be replaced with cornstarch, as written previously in this introduction. All pasta can be substituted with rice-based pasta.

Pantry Shopping List

This is a list of the most commonly used ingredients in the recipes in this book. In testing the recipes, we found that by stocking up on many of these essentials, you should be able to prepare nearly any recipe in this book for under $15.00.

Spice Rack

Allspice, Ground

Bay Leaves

Black Pepper

Chili Powder

Cinnamon, Ground

Cumin, Ground

Garlic Powder

Italian Seasoning

Nutmeg, Ground

Onion Powder

Paprika

Poultry Seasoning

Rosemary

Salt

Thyme

Cupboard

All-Purpose Flour

Apple Cider Vinegar

Balsamic Vinegar

Barbecue Sauce

Beef Base or Broth

Chicken Base or Broth

Chili Sauce

Chunky Salsa

Cornstarch

Diced Tomatoes, Canned

Dijon Mustard

Evaporated Milk

Ketchup

Light Brown Sugar

Minced Garlic, Jarred

Olive Oil

Red Wine Vinegar

Spaghetti Sauce, Jarred

Sugar

Tomato Paste

Vanilla Extract

Vegetable Oil

White Rice, Long-Grain

Worcestershire Sauce

Fridge

Bell Peppers

Butter or Margarine

Carrots

Celery

Cream Cheese

Eggs

Fresh Herbs

Frozen Corn Kernels

Frozen Peas

Parmesan Cheese, Grated

Red Onions

Tomatoes

Yellow Onions (Sweet)

Entertaining

Arugula and Artichoke Dip

A Unique Twist on a Favorite Dip

Everyone loves to dig their chips into spinach and artichoke dip, especially when it is kept warm inside the crock of a slow cooker. Of course, this recipe substitutes peppery arugula in place of spinach for something that is not only more refined, but more flavorful as well.

Shopping List

1 small red onion, diced

2 packed cups arugula leaves

16 ounces marinated artichoke hearts, drained and chopped

2 (8-ounce) bricks cream cheese, softened

½ cup mayonnaise

½ cup grated Asiago cheese (may use Parmesan)

2 teaspoons minced garlic

¼ cup finely diced red bell pepper

½ teaspoon salt

¼ teaspoon pepper

1 PLACE onion in a lightly greased skillet over medium-high heat and sauté until lightly caramelized, about 5 minutes. (You can also do this right in the crock of many modern slow cookers by using the cooker's browning function.)

2 PLACE caramelized onion in a slow cooker and cover with remaining ingredients, folding to combine.

3 SET the cooker to LOW, cover, and let cook 2 hours, or until hot and bubbly.

4 STIR well and set cooker to WARM before serving right out of the cooker. If dip is too thick, or thickens over time, thin out with a few tablespoons of milk.

Cut the Fat

Reduced-fat cream cheese and reduced-fat mayonnaise can be used in place of the full-fat varieties listed in the Shopping List, with almost no difference in flavor or texture.

Cranberry Meatballs

My Take on a Slow Cooker Prerequisite

Cranberry Meatballs are probably the single-most popular slow cooker recipe behind the traditional pot roast, so I knew I had to bring something new to this classic. While most recipes are made with jellied cranberry sauce, I use whole berry sauce and add bell pepper, garlic, and orange zest for zing. My biggest secret is the addition of soy sauce to offset the sweetness of the cranberry sauce.

Shopping List

32 ounces frozen meatballs

1 yellow onion, diced

1 green bell pepper, diced

1 (15-ounce) can whole berry
 cranberry sauce (not jellied)

1 cup chili sauce

1 teaspoon minced garlic

2 teaspoons soy sauce

2 teaspoons orange zest

1 ADD all ingredients to a slow cooker and toss to combine.

2 SET the cooker to LOW, cover, and let cook 6 hours, or until meatballs are hot throughout and you are ready to serve.

3 STIR well and set cooker to WARM before serving right out of the cooker, garnished with additional orange zest, if desired.

Make It Different

You can turn this into a recipe for Sweet and Sour Meatballs by omitting the cranberry sauce, adding an additional ½ cup of chili sauce, and adding 1 drained (20-ounce) can of pineapple chunks.

Party Cocktail Franks

My Unique Recipe for a Slow Cooker Classic

These sweet n' spicy weenies may cause quite a stir at any family event or friendly function where they're served. Don't be too surprised when they disappear before your very eyes.

Shopping List

2 (16-ounce) packages cocktail franks

1 cup barbecue sauce

1 cup chili sauce

½ cup apricot preserves

½ teaspoon chili powder

1 PLACE all ingredients in the crock of a slow cooker and stir to combine.

2 SET the cooker to LOW, cover, and let cook 2½–3 hours, or until sauce is bubbling hot.

3 SERVE hot, right out of the cooker.

Helpful Hint

In a pinch, you can also cook this recipe in about 4 minutes in the microwave, and simply use the slow cooker to keep them warm throughout your party.

Reuben Dip

The Deli Sandwich Favorite . . . in a Dip?

I must admit that I was unaware that Reuben Dip existed until I mentioned to someone that I was working on this cookbook. They insisted that I try it, and shared their recipe with me. I was pleasantly surprised, but worked on developing my own version with slightly less fat (by omitting Thousand Island dressing and using reduced-fat cream cheese in place of regular). My addition of allspice also enhances the pickled flavor of the corned beef.

Shopping List

¾ pound chopped corned beef

32 ounces sauerkraut, drained well

1 (8-ounce) brick reduced-fat
    cream cheese, softened

1½ cups shredded Swiss cheese

½ cup milk

¼ cup ketchup

3 tablespoons sweet relish

⅛ teaspoon ground allspice

1 ADD all ingredients to a slow cooker and toss to combine.

2 SET the cooker to LOW, cover, and let cook 2 hours, or until hot and bubbly.

3 STIR well and set cooker to WARM before serving right out of the cooker. If the dip is too thick, or thickens over time, simply add a few tablespoons of milk to thin it out.

4 SERVE alongside rye Melba toasts or hearty whole-grain crackers, for dipping.

Helpful Tip

Leftover corned beef is the best way to prepare this recipe, though you may also find precooked corned beef in the grocery store near the refrigerated tubs of prepared side dishes. You can also get corned beef from the deli counter and ask for it to be sliced extra thick.

Overnight Oatmeal

Enough to Serve a Crowd

With the aroma of cinnamon, vanilla, and brown sugar wafting in, it would be difficult to not immediately jump out from under the covers. Breakfast, in this instance, is waiting for you and not the other way around.

Shopping List

2 cups steel-cut oats

1 (12-ounce) can evaporated milk

6 cups water

¾ cup dried fruit

¼ cup light brown sugar

½ teaspoon vanilla extract

½ teaspoon ground cinnamon

⅛ teaspoon salt

1 PLACE all ingredients in the crock of a slow cooker and stir to combine.

2 SET cooker to LOW, cover, and let cook 8 hours, or until mixture is creamy and oats are tender.

3 SERVE with additional brown sugar to taste or drizzle with maple syrup for even more flavor!

Make It Yours

Any dried fruit works well in this oatmeal, so I'd suggest buying a bagged mix of dried berries. Otherwise, I especially like chopped dates or apricots.

Asian Pork Meatballs

With Sweet and Tangy Hoisin Sauce

These ground pork meatballs are filled with minced green onions and ginger to give you all the flavors in the filling of Asian potstickers. The savory meatballs are then cooked in a sweet hoisin sauce to make an unforgettable party appetizer.

Shopping List

MEATBALLS

2 pounds ground pork

½ cup panko bread crumbs

½ cup finely minced green onions

1 large egg

2 teaspoons minced garlic

½ teaspoon ground ginger

½ teaspoon salt

½ teaspoon pepper

SAUCE

1 (12-ounce) bottle hoisin sauce

1 cup beef stock or broth

2 teaspoons sesame oil

½ teaspoon onion powder

1 COMBINE all ingredients for MEATBALLS, using your hands to form into meatballs that are about the size of a silver dollar.

2 LOOSELY place the meatballs into a slow cooker, being careful not to press them down and into each other.

3 COMBINE all SAUCE ingredients and pour over top of the meatballs in the cooker.

4 SET the cooker to HIGH, cover, and let cook 3 hours.

5 SET the cooker to LOW or WARM and serve the meatballs right out of the cooker.

Helpful Hint

Hoisin sauce is sold in the Asian foods section of the grocery store near the soy sauce. It is tangy, sweet, and a lot like an Asian barbecue sauce.

Savory Snack Mix

My Favorite Mix, Made Easy

Put a bowl of this mix out on your counter or coffee table, and people will wonder what brand you're buying. It's simply more fun to just smile and say that it's a secret.

Shopping List

4 cups Corn Chex cereal

2 cups Wheat Chex cereal

2 cups mini pretzels

1½ cups square cheese crackers

1 cup roasted cashews

3 tablespoons butter, melted

⅔ of 1 (1-ounce) envelope powdered ranch dressing mix

1 teaspoon Worcestershire sauce

½ teaspoon chili powder

1 teaspoon paprika

1 PLACE Corn Chex, Wheat Chex, pretzels, cheese crackers, and cashews into the crock of a slow cooker.

2 WHISK together remaining ingredients and drizzle over the snack mix in the slow cooker, tossing to lightly coat all.

3 SET the cooker to LOW, cover, and let cook 1 hour.

4 UNCOVER, stir, and let cook uncovered 1 additional hour.

5 SPREAD on a sheet pan and let cool at least 15 minutes before serving. Store in an airtight container.

Make It Yours

Any combination of Rice, Corn, or Wheat Chex cereal will work, though I find that the Rice Chex can get a little soggy. Mixed nuts or dry roasted peanuts can be used in place of the more expensive cashews.

Pizza Dip

A New Party Favorite

Put this appetizer out and people will line up, as it offers everything delivery does, only on a chip, saving room for the main course. And let's face it . . . much like bacon, cream cheese makes everything even better.

Shopping List

2 teaspoons olive oil

1 small red onion, diced

½ cup diced green bell pepper

2 (8-ounce) bricks cream cheese, cubed

12 ounces pizza sauce

¾ cup grated Parmesan cheese

⅓ cup sliced black olives

1 teaspoon Italian seasoning

¼ teaspoon garlic powder

¼ teaspoon salt

1 PLACE olive oil and onion in a skillet over medium-high heat and sauté until lightly caramelized, about 5 minutes. (You can also do this right in the crock of many modern slow cookers by using the cooker's browning function.)

2 ADD diced bell pepper to the skillet and sauté just 1 minute longer.

3 TRANSFER caramelized onion and bell pepper to a slow cooker and cover with remaining ingredients, folding to combine.

4 SET the cooker to LOW, cover, and let cook 2 hours, or until hot and bubbly.

5 STIR well, and set cooker to WARM before serving right out of the cooker.

Make It Better

Sliced turkey pepperoni (8 ounces) can be chopped and added to the dip before cooking for even more great pizza taste. Using regular pepperoni is not recommended, as too much grease will cook out and into the dip.

Swedish Meatballs

In a Tarragon Cream Sauce

While these appetizing meatballs can be devoured in one bite, they can also be served as an entrée. The traditional approach to seasoning certainly leaves none the wiser to the fact they're actually frozen. So long as you don't tell, neither will I.

Shopping List

32 ounces frozen meatballs

1 cup beef stock or broth

1 green bell pepper, diced

½ cup diced yellow onion

2 teaspoons minced garlic

1½ teaspoons onion powder

¼ teaspoon nutmeg

½ teaspoon allspice

1 tablespoon dry or fresh tarragon
leaves (may use parsley)

16 ounces sour cream

Salt and pepper to taste

1 ADD all ingredients, except for sour cream, to a slow cooker and toss to combine.

2 SET the cooker to LOW, cover, and let cook 6 hours, or until meatballs are hot throughout, and you are ready to serve.

3 TURN off heat, stir in sour cream, and season with salt and pepper to taste. Serve with toothpicks at a party, or over buttered noodles as an entrée.

Helpful Hints

Regular frozen meatballs (not Italian-style) work best in this recipe. To lower the fat, turkey meatballs and reduced-fat sour cream can be substituted.

Black Bean Queso Dip

Creamy, Chunky, and Everything You'd Want on a Chip

Slow cookers are a party staple for their ability to keep appetizers like this chunky black bean and cheese dip warm all night long. Simply give it a quick stir every so often and you'll have a hit from the first chip to the last.

Shopping List

2 (15-ounce) cans black beans, drained and rinsed

1 (8-ounce) brick reduced-fat cream cheese, softened

8 ounces pasteurized cheese (such as Velvceta)

1 cup chunky salsa

1 teaspoon chili powder

¼ teaspoon salt

⅛ teaspoon pepper

1 ADD all ingredients to a slow cooker and toss to combine.

2 SET the cooker to LOW, cover, and let cook 2 hours, or until hot and bubbly.

3 STIR well and set cooker to WARM before serving right out of the cooker.

Make It Different

For even more flavor, add ½ teaspoon of ground cumin and 2 tablespoons of fresh chopped cilantro in Step 1.

Cajun Mixed Nuts

A Unique Coffee Table Snack

These warm and crunchy mixed nuts have just the right amount of Cajun spice. There's nothing like them, especially when eaten fresh, right out of the cooker.

Shopping List

2 cups raw almonds

2 cups raw pecans

3 tablespoons butter or margarine, melted

2 teaspoons light brown sugar

1 teaspoon Worcestershire sauce

1 teaspoon paprika

½ teaspoon chili powder

½ teaspoon onion powder

¼ teaspoon garlic powder

⅛ teaspoon cayenne pepper

½ teaspoon salt

⅛ teaspoon black pepper

2 cups roasted cashews

1 PLACE all ingredients, except cashews, in slow cooker and toss to evenly coat nuts with butter and seasonings.

2 SET the cooker to LOW, cover, and let cook 2 hours.

3 UNCOVER, stir in cashews, and let cook uncovered 1 additional hour, or until almonds are crunchy and roasted.

4 SERVE warm or room temperature. (They're best when they're fresh and hot out of the cooker.)

Helpful Hint

Raw almonds and pecans are usually found in the baking aisle near the bags of chocolate chips, though they are sometimes sold in the produce section as well.

Prep Time	Cook Time	Temperature	Serves
15 min	2 hrs	Low	12

Creamy Crab Dip

Take a Dip in Chesapeake Bay

Any seafood lover can appreciate the rich texture of crab, and while a trip to the Northeast isn't necessary for this appetizing dip, a slow cooker sure is—keeping it warm and creamy until the party is over.

Shopping List

2 teaspoons olive oil

1 small yellow onion, diced

1½ (8-ounce) bricks cream cheese, cubed

1 cup reduced-fat mayonnaise

2 (6-ounce) cans crabmeat, drained

½ cup grated Parmesan cheese

1 tablespoon lemon juice

1 teaspoon Tabasco Sauce

1¼ teaspoons Old Bay Seasoning

1 teaspoon minced garlic

½ teaspoon salt

¼ teaspoon pepper

1 PLACE olive oil and onion in a skillet over medium-high heat, and sauté until lightly caramelized, about 5 minutes. (You can also do this right in the crock of many modern slow cookers by using the cooker's browning function.)

2 TRANSFER caramelized onion to a slow cooker and cover with remaining ingredients, folding to combine.

3 SET the cooker to LOW, cover, and let cook 2 hours, or until hot and bubbly.

4 STIR well and set cooker to WARM before serving right out of the cooker.

Make It Better

Try stirring in 1 cup of shredded sharp Cheddar cheese and 1 tablespoon of chopped flat-leaf parsley in the last 30 minutes of cooking for even more flavor.

Barbecue Chicken Wings

Kept Warm in the Slow Cooker

When the weather is clear, there's no better time to spark up that grill, though these wings require absolutely no coals, fuel, or flame to achieve that smoky barbecue flavor that we've come to know and love. Just don't forget the wet-naps!

Shopping List

3 pounds chicken wings, wings and drums separated

Salt and pepper to taste

1 (12-ounce) bottle ketchup

3 tablespoons red wine vinegar

¼ cup dark brown sugar

1 tablespoon Worcestershire sauce

2 tablespoons yellow mustard

½ teaspoon liquid smoke

½ teaspoon onion powder

¼ teaspoon garlic powder

1 PREHEAT broiler and generously season chicken with salt and pepper.

2 PLACE chicken on a broiler pan and broil on top rack of oven for 5–7 minutes on each side, just until golden brown.

3 MEANWHILE, add all remaining ingredients to a slow cooker and stir to combine.

4 TRANSFER broiled chicken to the sauce in the cooker, tossing all to coat.

5 SET the cooker to LOW, cover, and let cook 3–4 hours, or until meat is tender and drumettes are cooked throughout.

Make It Different

Make a less messy party appetizer by using boneless, skinless chicken thighs in place of the wings. Simply slice each thigh into 3 thick strips before Step 1.

Quick Pizza Dough

Because Dough Loves a Warm Place to Rise

Making a perfect, crispy-crusted pizza might be the last thing you'd think of doing with a slow cooker—and while actually cooking that pizza in the cooker isn't possible—few people realize that slow cookers are the absolute perfect place to let dough rise. This recipe makes enough dough for two 12-inch pies.

Shopping List

1½ cups warm water

1 envelope rapid rising yeast

2 teaspoons sugar

3½ cups bread flour

2 tablespoons olive oil

1½ teaspoons salt

Cornmeal, for dusting

Your favorite pizza sauce and toppings

Make It Easier

You can also use a rolling pin to roll the dough out, though the shape might not be perfectly round. (It's the taste that counts anyway!)

1 IN a small mixing bowl, combine warm water, yeast, and sugar. Let stand 5 minutes.

2 ADD bread flour, olive oil, and salt to a large mixing bowl.

3 POUR the water and yeast mixture into the flour mixture and knead until a firm dough has formed. If dough is sticky, knead in additional flour a few pinches at a time. Form dough into a ball.

4 SPRAY a slow cooker with nonstick cooking spray and set to HIGH for only 5 minutes.

5 TURN slow cooker off entirely. Place ball of dough inside and cover immediately. Let dough rise 45–60 minutes.

6 ONCE dough has risen, divide into 2 pieces. Flour a surface and use your fingers to stretch and pull each piece into a round crust. Push from the center out to stretch each piece of dough until about 12 inches in diameter.

7 TOP with your favorite pizza sauce and toppings, and place on round or sheet pans dusted with cornmeal to prevent sticking. Bake in an oven preheated to 450° for 12–15 minutes, or until toppings are browned and crust is crispy.

Soups
and Stews

All Day Chili

You Chill While It Cooks

Chili is one of the biggest slow cooker staples, getting even better the longer it simmers. In this version, ground sirloin is called for, and while out West, they typically don't include beans, I personally prefer the added texture.

Shopping List

1 tablespoon olive oil

2 pounds ground sirloin

1 yellow onion, chopped

1 (14½-ounce) can diced tomatoes, undrained

1 (15-ounce) can kidney beans, drained and rinsed

1 (8-ounce) can tomato sauce

1 cup beef stock or broth

1 green bell pepper, chopped

1 tablespoon minced garlic

1 tablespoon chili powder

2 teaspoons cornmeal

½ teaspoon cumin

1 teaspoon salt

½ teaspoon pepper

1 PLACE olive oil and ground sirloin in a large skillet over medium-high heat, browning well, about 5 minutes. (You can also do this right in the crock of many modern slow cookers by using the cooker's browning function.)

2 WHEN meat is almost browned, drain off any excess fat, return to heat, and add onions, cooking just until they begin to sweat.

3 TRANSFER browned meat and onions to a slow cooker and cover with remaining ingredients, stirring to combine.

4 SET the cooker to LOW, cover, and let cook 8 hours before serving.

Helpful Tip

Any kind of ground beef may be used in place of the ground sirloin; just be sure to drain off excess grease.

Broccoli, Chicken, and Cheese Soup

With Potatoes, Too . . . Why Not?

This soup was first inspired by Chicken Divan, a traditional casserole dish with chicken, broccoli, and creamy Mornay cheese sauce. The addition of potatoes makes this into a hearty dish fit for a meal.

Shopping List

2 tablespoons butter or margarine

1 pound boneless, skinless chicken breasts, chopped

1 yellow onion, diced

20 ounces frozen broccoli florets

6 baby red potatoes, chopped

3½ cups chicken stock or broth

¼ teaspoon poultry seasoning

½ teaspoon salt

½ teaspoon pepper

3 tablespoons all-purpose flour

1 cup whole milk

2 cups shredded sharp Cheddar cheese

1 MELT butter in a skillet over medium-high heat. Add chicken and onion, and sauté until chicken is browned and onion begins to caramelize, about 5 minutes. (You can also do this right in the crock of many modern slow cookers by using the cooker's browning function.)

2 PLACE browned chicken and onion in a slow cooker and cover with broccoli, potatoes, chicken stock, poultry seasoning, salt, and pepper. Stir to combine.

3 SET the cooker to LOW, cover, and let cook 6 hours.

4 WHISK flour into milk, and stir into soup. Re-cover, set the cooker to HIGH, and let cook 1 additional hour.

5 TURN off heat and add Cheddar cheese, stirring just until melted and combined. Serve immediately.

Make It Faster

Pre-cut potato cubes (Simply Potatoes brand) can sometimes be found near the eggs in your grocer's refrigerated case. Purchasing this and pre-diced onion can significantly cut down on prep time.

Seasonal Beef Stew

With Sweet Potatoes and Green Apples

Who would have thought sweet potatoes and tart apples could play so well with a beef roast? Though these flavors are typically reserved for pork (and you could definitely substitute a pork roast in a pinch), they truly make for something entirely new when paired with beef.

Shopping List

1 (3- to 4-pound) beef chuck roast, cut into 1-inch cubes

Salt and pepper to taste

2 tablespoons olive oil

3 cups beef stock or broth

4 sweet potatoes, peeled and cut into 2-inch cubes

2 green apples, cored and cut into wedges

2 large onions, chopped

1 cup diced celery

3 tablespoons balsamic vinegar

¼ cup tomato paste

1 teaspoon dried rosemary

½ teaspoon ground allspice

¼ teaspoon cinnamon

1 teaspoon salt

¼ teaspoon pepper

1 tablespoon cornstarch

1 GENEROUSLY season the cubed beef with salt and pepper.

2 PLACE olive oil in a skillet over high heat, until nearly smoking hot. Add seasoned beef, and brown on all sides. (You can also do this right in the crock of many modern slow cookers by using the cooker's browning function.)

3 REMOVE skillet from heat and deglaze pan with the beef stock, scraping any browned bits from the bottom.

4 TRANSFER beef and all liquid from the skillet to a slow cooker, and top with remaining ingredients, except cornstarch.

5 SET the cooker to LOW, cover, and let cook 5 hours.

6 WHISK cornstarch into 2 tablespoons of water and stir into the cooking liquid. Re-cover, set the cooker to HIGH, and let cook 1 additional hour or until meat is fork-tender.

Make It Different

Butternut squash works great in place of the sweet potatoes in this recipe.

New England Clam Chowder

Creamy Chowder That Cooks Itself

New England Clam Chowder is an extremely simple recipe but can be tricky when prepared traditionally, as you need to constantly stir it and regulate the temperature to prevent the cream from burning. My recipe uses evaporated milk, which is far less likely to burn, especially when cooking slow and low in a slow cooker.

Shopping List

4 slices bacon, chopped

1 yellow onion, diced

3 stalks celery, diced

3 (6-ounce) cans baby clams, undrained

4 cups peeled and cubed potatoes

3 tablespoons butter or margarine

3 tablespoons all-purpose flour

2 (12-ounce) cans evaporated milk

¼ teaspoon dried thyme

1 teaspoon salt

½ teaspoon pepper

1 PLACE bacon in a skillet over medium-high heat and cook until it fully greases the pan. Add onion and celery and cook until bacon begins to crisp and onions begin to caramelize. (You can also do this right in the crock of many modern slow cookers by using the cooker's browning function.)

2 TRANSFER bacon and vegetables to a slow cooker and top with undrained clams, potatoes, and butter.

3 WHISK together flour, evaporated milk, thyme, salt, and pepper and pour over all in the cooker.

4 SET the cooker to LOW, cover, and let cook 8 hours, or until potatoes are tender.

Helpful Hint

To further thicken the broth, uncover in the last hour of cooking and raise the temperature from LOW to HIGH.

Chicken and Sweet Corn Chowder

With Bacon and Bell Pepper

In my last (pressure cooking) book I had a recipe for a corn soup that was so good that I knew I wanted to expand upon it and turn it into a chowder worthy of a full meal. This recipe is not only creamier and thicker than my previous recipe, but adds chicken and bacon to make this a true entrée.

Shopping List

1 pound boneless, skinless chicken breasts, cubed

2 tablespoons all-purpose flour

Salt and pepper to taste

3 slices bacon, chopped

1 small yellow onion, diced

½ cup diced red bell pepper

24 ounces frozen corn kernels

1 cup chicken stock or broth

2 (12-ounce) cans evaporated milk

2 tablespoons butter or margarine

1 tablespoon sugar

1 teaspoon salt

½ teaspoon dried thyme

3 tablespoons cornstarch

1 Toss the cubed chicken breasts in flour that has been generously seasoned with salt and pepper.

2 PLACE bacon in a skillet over medium-high heat, and cook until it fully greases the pan. Add floured chicken, and brown both the chicken and bacon, about 5 minutes. (You can also do this right in the crock of many modern slow cookers by using the cooker's browning function.)

3 TRANSFER chicken and bacon to a slow cooker and top with all remaining ingredients, except cornstarch.

4 SET the cooker to LOW, cover, and let cook 6 hours.

5 SET cooker to HIGH, whisk cornstarch into 3 tablespoons of water and add to the chowder. Let cook 1 additional hour or until thickened.

Helpful Hint

For an even heartier chowder you can add 2 chopped potatoes in Step 3.

Black Bean Chili

With Corn and Cilantro

I've always been a huge fan of slow cooker chili for one main reason: there are countless ways to approach it. This approach goes more Tex-Mex than the other chili recipes in this book.

Shopping List

1 tablespoon olive oil

1 pound lean ground beef

1 large red onion, chopped

1 (14½-ounce) can diced tomatoes, undrained

2 (15-ounce) cans black beans, drained and rinsed

1 (8-ounce) can tomato sauce

1 cup beef stock or broth

3 tablespoons tomato paste

1 tablespoon minced garlic

2 tablespoons chili powder

2 teaspoons ground cumin

1 teaspoon salt

½ teaspoon pepper

¾ cup frozen corn kernels

¼ cup chopped cilantro

1 PLACE olive oil and ground beef in a large skillet over medium-high heat, browning well, about 5 minutes. (You can also do this right in the crock of many modern slow cookers by using the cooker's browning function.)

2 WHEN meat is almost browned, drain off any excess grease, return to heat, and add onion, cooking just until they sweat.

3 TRANSFER all to the slow cooker and cover with remaining ingredients, except corn and cilantro, stirring to combine.

4 SET the cooker to LOW, cover, and let cook 6 hours. Stir in corn and cilantro 30 minutes before serving.

Make It Better

Cubed beef stew meat can be used in place of the lean ground beef for an even heartier and unique chili.

Italian Sausage Wedding Soup

You Won't Miss the Mini Meatballs!

The hardest part of making traditional Italian Wedding Soup is rolling out dozens of tiny meatballs by hand. This recipe forgoes that tedious process, replacing the meatballs with flavorful Italian sausage crumbles for something that is not only easier, but much more rustic.

Shopping List

1 tablespoon olive oil

1 pound ground Italian sausage, no casings

1 red onion, diced

2 carrots, sliced

6 cups chicken stock or broth

4 packed cups chopped kale

1 teaspoon lemon juice

2 teaspoons minced garlic

1 bay leaf

¼ teaspoon crushed red pepper flakes

½ cup small pasta

Salt and pepper to taste

Shredded Parmesan cheese, to serve

1 PLACE olive oil in a large skillet over medium-high heat. Add ground sausage, and cook until brown, about 5 minutes. (You can also do this right in the crock of many modern slow cookers by using the cooker's browning function.)

2 WHEN meat is almost browned, drain off any excess fat, return to heat, and add onion and carrots, cooking just until the onions sweat.

3 TRANSFER browned meat and vegetables to a slow cooker. Add chicken broth, kale, lemon juice, garlic, bay leaf, and crushed red pepper and stir to combine.

4 SET the cooker to LOW, cover, and let cook 6 hours, adding the pasta in the last hour of cooking.

5 SEASON with salt and pepper to taste and serve each bowl topped with a sprinkling of shredded Parmesan cheese.

Helpful Hint

"Acini de pepe" is the typical round pasta found in Italian Wedding Soup, but any small pasta such as ditalini, orecchiette, or even orzo will work well in this recipe.

Autumn Turkey Chili

With Pumpkin and Fall Spices

The canned pumpkin in this recipe may seem strange at first, but it actually thickens the chili and absorbs the flavors of all the spices and other ingredients as things slowly cook.

Shopping List

2 tablespoons vegetable oil

1 pound ground turkey

1 yellow onion, chopped

1 (14½-ounce) can diced tomatoes, undrained

1 (15-ounce) can pumpkin

1 (15-ounce) can Great Northern beans, drained and rinsed

⅔ cup chicken stock or broth

2 teaspoons minced garlic

2 teaspoons chili powder

2 teaspoons sugar

½ teaspoon cumin

¼ teaspoon ground cinnamon

¼ teaspoon ground allspice

1 pinch nutmeg

¾ teaspoon salt

¼ teaspoon pepper

1 PLACE vegetable oil in a large skillet over medium-high heat. Add ground turkey, and cook until brown, about 5 minutes. (You can also do this right in the crock of many modern slow cookers by using the cooker's browning function.)

2 WHEN meat is almost browned, drain off any excess fat, return to heat, and add onion, cooking just until they sweat.

3 TRANSFER browned meat and onion to a slow cooker and cover with remaining ingredients, stirring to combine.

4 SET the cooker to LOW, cover, and let cook 8 hours before serving.

Make It Better

Serve this topped with plain Greek yogurt and a fine drizzle of real maple syrup for just a touch of sweetness.

Chicken Noodle Soup

Because This Wouldn't Be a Soup Section Without It

It's hard to improve upon Chicken Noodle Soup, but making it in the slow cooker definitely improves upon cooking it. The chicken comes out tender every time and you are free to leave your house without the worry of leaving the stove unattended.

Shopping List

1 pound boneless, skinless chicken breasts, cubed

2 tablespoons all-purpose flour

Salt and pepper to taste

2 tablespoons butter or margarine

6 cups chicken stock or broth

1 yellow onion, diced

4 ribs celery, sliced

3 large carrots, sliced

1 teaspoon dried marjoram

½ teaspoon dried thyme

1 bay leaf

½ teaspoon salt

¼ teaspoon pepper

8 ounces uncooked egg noodles

1 Toss the cubed chicken breasts in flour that has been generously seasoned with salt and pepper.

2 PLACE butter in a skillet over medium-high heat, until sizzling. Add floured chicken, and brown on both sides, about 5 minutes. (You can also do this right in the crock of many modern slow cookers by using the cooker's browning function.)

3 TRANSFER chicken to a slow cooker and top with all remaining ingredients, except egg noodles.

4 SET the cooker to LOW, cover, and let cook 6 hours.

5 SET cooker to HIGH, add egg noodles, and cook 1 additional hour before serving.

Make It Better

A satchel of fresh herbs can be used in place of the dried marjoram, thyme, and bay leaf. They sometimes sell a "poultry" mix of fresh herbs in the produce section that works perfectly.

Sausage and Lentil Soup

Robust Italian Flavors in a Bowl

You don't have to wait until the leaves fall to enjoy this autumn favorite packed with healthy lentils, veggies, and Italian sausage. Thankfully, you don't have to fly to Italy either!

Shopping List

2 teaspoons vegetable oil

1 pound ground Italian sausage (no casings)

1 large yellow onion, chopped

2 carrots, diced

2 tomatoes, diced

8 cups beef stock or broth

8 ounces dried lentils

3 tablespoons tomato paste

2 bay leaves

1 teaspoon Italian seasoning

¾ teaspoon salt

½ teaspoon pepper

1 PLACE vegetable oil in a skillet over medium-high heat.

2 ADD ground sausage to the hot skillet, and sauté until browned, about 5 minutes. Add onion, carrots, and tomatoes, and toss to combine. Remove from heat. (You can also sauté right in the crock of many modern slow cookers by using the cooker's browning function.)

3 PLACE browned meat and vegetables in a slow cooker and cover with remaining ingredients, stirring to combine.

4 SET the cooker to LOW, cover, and let cook 6–8 hours, or until lentils are tender.

Make It Better

Add ½ cup of diced roasted red bell pepper just before serving to add contrasting color and flavor.

Beef and Barley Stew

It's Hard to Beat a Classic Like This

You simply can't go wrong with this classic stew. Barley—with its nutty flavor and chewy texture—makes for a nice change from traditional starches like pasta or potatoes.

Shopping List

2 teaspoons vegetable oil

1 pound cubed beef stew meat

1 tablespoon all-purpose flour

Salt and pepper to taste

1 yellow onion, diced

3 carrots, chopped

3 stalks celery, chopped

6 cups beef stock or broth

1 (14½-ounce) can diced tomatoes, undrained

2 bay leaves

2 teaspoons minced garlic

1 teaspoon dried thyme

½ teaspoon onion powder

½ cup "quick cooking" barley

1 cup frozen green beans

Make It Better

After browning the beef, deglaze the pan with a little of the beef broth, scraping any browned bits to pour into the soup.

1 PLACE vegetable oil in a skillet over medium-high heat. Toss beef stew meat in flour that has been seasoned with a pinch of salt and pepper.

2 ADD seasoned stew meat to the hot skillet, and sauté until browned, about 5 minutes. Add onion, carrots, and celery and toss to combine. Remove from heat. (You can also sauté right in the crock of many modern slow cookers by using the cooker's browning function.)

3 PLACE browned meat and vegetables in a slow cooker and cover with beef broth, diced tomatoes, bay leaves, garlic, thyme, and onion powder.   Stir to combine.

4 SET the cooker to LOW, cover, and let cook 7 hours.

5 STIR in barley and green beans. Re-cover and let cook 1 additional hour.

6 SEASON with salt and pepper to taste before serving.

Split Pea and Canadian Bacon Soup

A Healthier Twist on a Classic

Split pea soup is usually flavored by the addition of fatty ham hocks that melt into the soup as it cooks, but my recipe uses lean Canadian bacon instead. Honestly though, that was just an added benefit, as I first started making this soup this way when I couldn't find ham hocks at the grocery store and have loved it ever since.

Shopping List

1 pound dried split peas

8 ounces Canadian bacon, diced

1 yellow onion, diced

3 carrots, diced

8 cups chicken stock or broth

2 teaspoons minced garlic

2 bay leaves

½ teaspoon onion powder

¼ teaspoon dried marjoram

Salt and pepper to taste

1 ADD all ingredients to a slow cooker and stir to combine.

2 SET the cooker to HIGH, cover, and let cook 5 hours.

3 SEASON with salt and pepper to taste before serving.

Helpful Hint

For a thicker broth, use a potato masher to mash the cooked split peas into the broth until the desired consistency is achieved.

Chili Verde

Green Chili with Ground Turkey

This green chili with plenty of tomatillos, white beans, chiles, and cilantro will brighten up your day and put a kick in your step.

Shopping List

2 teaspoons vegetable oil

1 pound ground turkey

1 large yellow onion, chopped

1 green bell pepper, diced

4 cups chicken stock or broth

8 tomatillos, husked and chopped

2 (15-ounce) cans white beans (Great Northern or cannellini), drained

2 (4-ounce) cans diced green chiles

1 tablespoon minced garlic

1 teaspoon ground cumin

½ teaspoon coriander

1 teaspoon salt

½ teaspoon pepper

⅓ cup chopped cilantro

1 PLACE vegetable oil in a skillet over medium-high heat.

2 ADD ground turkey to the hot skillet, and sauté until browned, about 5 minutes. Add onion and bell pepper and toss to combine. Remove from heat. (You can also sauté right in the crock of many modern slow cookers by using the cooker's browning function.)

3 PLACE browned meat and vegetables in a slow cooker and cover with remaining ingredients, except cilantro. Stir to combine.

4 SET the cooker to LOW, cover, and let cook 8 hours.

5 STIR in cilantro before serving.

Make It Memorable

Serve this chili topped with a squeeze of fresh lime juice and a dollop of sour cream for the absolute perfect combination.

White Bean and Pesto Soup

Clean Italian Flavors in a Hearty Bean Soup

This soup with a base of white cannellini beans would be good enough on its own, but then it is topped with a large dollop of flavorful basil pesto. The pesto literally melts right into the soup as you eat, making for something that's not only delicious, but also well presented.

Shopping List

1 pound dried cannellini beans

1 yellow onion, diced

2 stalks celery, diced

6 cups chicken stock or broth

1 tablespoon olive oil

2 teaspoons minced garlic

1 teaspoon lemon juice

1 teaspoon dried thyme

Salt and pepper to taste

6 ounces prepared basil pesto

Helpful Hint

Though you can find basil pesto in jars near the pasta sauces, I prefer refrigerated pesto sold in the deli or near the refrigerated ravioli. Look for pesto with pine nuts in the ingredients for the best quality.

1 SOAK cannellini beans overnight by placing in a large bowl and covering with cold water. Leave at least 3 inches of water for the beans to expand.

2 DRAIN and rinse the soaked beans and place in a slow cooker.

3 ADD remaining ingredients, except pesto, and stir to combine.

4 SET the cooker to LOW, cover, and let cook 8 hours, or until beans are tender.

5 DRAIN off about ½ of any excess liquid, then use a potato masher or heavy spoon to mash ½ of the beans into the remaining liquid, thickening the soup.

6 SEASON with additional salt and pepper to taste, if desired.

7 SERVE each bowl of soup topped with a large spoonful of basil pesto.

Tuscan Ribollita

Robust Italian Soup Served over Crusty Bread

While ribollita is usually cooked with the bread right in the soup, I prefer to serve this soup with bread at the bottom of the bowl. This way the bread soaks up all the broth without breaking up into it.

Shopping List

1 pound dried cannellini beans

1 yellow onion, diced

2 carrots, sliced

2 stalks celery, sliced

8 cups chicken stock or broth

1 (6-ounce) can tomato paste

1 tomato, chopped

3 packed cups chopped kale

2 teaspoons minced garlic

1 bay leaf

1 teaspoon dried thyme

½ teaspoon dried oregano

Salt and pepper to taste

3 cups cubed Italian bread

Extra virgin olive oil, to serve

1 SOAK cannellini beans overnight by placing in a large bowl and covering with cold water. Leave at least 3 inches of water for the beans to expand.

2 DRAIN and rinse the soaked beans and place in a slow cooker.

3 ADD onion, carrots, celery, chicken broth, tomato paste, tomato, kale, garlic, bay leaf, thyme, and oregano to the cooker, and stir to combine.

4 SET the cooker to LOW, cover, and let cook 8 hours, or until beans are tender.

5 SEASON soup with salt and pepper to taste.

6 PLACE a handful of cubed bread in the bottom of each serving bowl and drizzle with olive oil. Ladle soup over the bread before serving.

Helpful Hint

You can make this into a full entrée soup by adding 1 pound of sliced boneless, skinless chicken thighs before cooking.

Italian Beef Stew

With Gnocchi Dumplings

I love gnocchi. Little Italian potato dumplings, gnocchi have only started to appear in grocery stores in the last few years, but they've appeared in a very big way. Now all of my local stores carry multiple brands and I couldn't be happier. This beef stew uses gnocchi in place of noodles or traditional drop dumplings for something totally unique without adding any extra prep work.

Shopping List

1 tablespoon olive oil

1 pound cubed beef stew meat

1 tablespoon all-purpose flour

Salt and pepper to taste

8 ounces sliced baby bella
   mushrooms

1 red onion, diced

3 carrots, chopped

6 cups beef stock or broth

1 (14½-ounce) can diced tomatoes,
   undrained

¼ cup dry red wine

1 bay leaf

1 tablespoon minced garlic

2 teaspoons Italian seasoning

1 (16-ounce) package dried
   gnocchi

1 PLACE olive oil in a skillet over medium-high heat. Toss beef stew meat in flour that has been seasoned with a pinch of salt and pepper.

2 ADD seasoned stew meat to the hot skillet, and sauté until browned, about 5 minutes. Add mushrooms, onion, and carrots, and toss to combine. Remove from heat. (You can also sauté right in the crock of many modern slow cookers by using the cooker's browning function.)

3 PLACE browned meat and vegetables in a slow cooker and cover with remaining ingredients, except gnocchi. Stir to combine.

4 SET the cooker to LOW, cover, and let cook 7 hours.

5 STIR in gnocchi. Re-cover and let cook 1 additional hour.

6 SEASON with salt and pepper to taste before serving.

Helpful Hint

Gnocchi is usually sold in vacuum-sealed packages in the pasta and rice aisle of the grocery store.

Slow Cooker
Casseroles

Corndog Casserole

My Take on Another Slow Cooker Classic

Variations on corndog casseroles like this one have been around for as long as I can remember, but this version is my personal favorite. You've got baked beans and hot dogs on the bottom and a cornbread topping—what's not to love?

Shopping List

2 (28-ounce) cans baked beans

1 pound hot dogs, sliced

½ cup diced yellow onion

2 tablespoons yellow mustard

1 (8½-ounce) package corn muffin mix

1 (15-ounce) can creamed corn

1 large egg, beaten

¼ cup all-purpose flour

2 tablespoons vegetable oil

1 pinch salt

1 PLACE baked beans, hot dogs, yellow onion, and mustard in a slow cooker and stir to combine.

2 FOLD together all remaining ingredients and spread over top hot dog and bean mixture in the slow cooker.

3 SET the cooker to LOW, cover, and let cook 6 hours.

4 UNCOVER and cook 1 additional hour, or until cornbread is cooked through.

Helpful Tips

Use your favorite variety of canned baked beans and favorite brand of hot dogs to tune this recipe to your liking. Or try using 2 cans of chili in place of the baked beans for something entirely different.

Paella

With Chicken, Ham, and Shrimp

This slow cooker re-creation of a classic Spanish dish with rice and saffron may seem intimidating at first, but it is a lot easier to prepare than you'd think. The depth of flavors that comes out as it slow cooks is nothing less than sublime.

Shopping List

2 tablespoons olive oil

1 pound boneless, skinless chicken thighs, sliced thick

1 yellow onion, diced

1 red bell pepper, diced

⅔ cup cubed ham

3¼ cups chicken stock or broth

1 (14½-ounce) can diced tomatoes, undrained

2 teaspoons minced garlic

1 bay leaf

1 teaspoon paprika

1 teaspoon dried oregano

½ teaspoon dried thyme

1 pinch saffron threads, crushed

¼ teaspoon cayenne pepper

1 teaspoon salt

1½ cups long-grain white rice, uncooked

8 ounces shrimp, peeled and deveined

1 PLACE olive oil in a skillet over high heat, until nearly smoking. Add chicken, and brown on both sides, about 5 minutes. Toss in onion and bell pepper and remove from heat. (You can also do this right in the crock of many modern slow cookers by using the cooker's browning function.)

2 TRANSFER the chicken and vegetables to a slow cooker and then top with remaining ingredients, except rice and shrimp.

3 SET the cooker to LOW, cover, and let cook 6 hours.

4 STIR in rice and cook an additional 1 hour and 45 minutes.

5 ADD shrimp and cook an additional 15 minutes before serving.

Helpful Hint

You can cut the chicken stock down to 1¼ cups and add 3 cups of cooked rice (sold frozen or in "Ready Rice" pouches) when you add the shrimp to let this cook unattended for nearly 8 hours.

Prep Time	Cook Time	Temperature	Serves
20 min	10 hrs	Low	10

Tater Breakfast Casserole

You Can Sleep In . . . Breakfast Made Itself

This breakfast casserole loaded with tater tots, ham, bell peppers, eggs, and cheese is more than enough to feed a crowd and feed them what they want! With a ten-hour cook time, preparing it the night before will leave no worries of it overcooking by the morning.

Shopping List

1 (32-ounce) bag frozen tater tots

1 pound cubed ham

1 yellow onion, diced

⅓ cup diced green bell pepper

⅓ cup diced red bell pepper

1 cup shredded sharp Cheddar cheese

12 large eggs

1 cup milk

¼ teaspoon garlic powder

1 teaspoon salt

¼ teaspoon pepper

1 PLACE ⅓ of the tater tots at the bottom of a slow cooker.

2 TOP potatoes with ⅓ of the ham, onion, and bell peppers. Then top that with ⅓ of the cheese.

3 REPEAT this process 2 more times to make 3 layers in all.

4 WHISK together eggs, milk, garlic powder, salt, and pepper. Pour over top of all in slow cooker.

5 SET the cooker to LOW, cover, and let cook 10 hours.

Make It Better

I like to add a few drops of Tabasco Sauce to the egg mixture in Step 4 to give things a little kick.

Ravioli Lasagna

Made with Only Five Non-Pantry Ingredients

This Ravioli Lasagna is the easier of the two lasagna recipes in this book. In fact, it's so easy that it only includes five non-pantry ingredients. Rather than layer the pasta and ricotta cheese separately, frozen cheese-filled raviolis are used to fill both roles at the same time.

Shopping List

1 tablespoon olive oil

1 yellow onion, diced

1 pound lean ground beef

Salt and pepper to taste

1 (24-ounce) jar chunky spaghetti sauce

1 (25-ounce) bag frozen cheese ravioli

2 cups shredded mozzarella cheese

1 HEAT olive oil in a large skillet over high heat. Add onion, ground beef, and a pinch of salt and pepper. Sauté until meat is browned.

2 STIR spaghetti sauce into the ground beef mixture, and remove from heat.

3 SPOON ¼ of the beef and sauce mixture into the bottom of a slow cooker and then cover with a layer of ⅓ of the frozen ravioli.

4 TOP the frozen ravioli with another layer of sauce, then ⅓ of the mozzarella cheese.

5 REPEAT for 2 more layers of ravioli, then sauce, then cheese, ending with the cheese on top.

6 SET the cooker to LOW, cover, and let cook 7 hours, or until raviolis are hot throughout.

Helpful Hint

Using fresh ravioli from the refrigerated (not frozen) case is not recommended, as the pasta can fall apart after extended cooking.

Jambalaya

With Smoked Sausage and Shrimp

This Creole cousin to Spanish paella can be made with countless combinations of meat, sausage, and seafood. My version is as simple and easy as it gets, using only sausage and shrimp to save money while keeping all of the most important flavors intact.

Shopping List

2 tablespoons butter or margarine

2 stalks celery, sliced

1 yellow onion, diced

1 green bell pepper, diced

8 ounces smoked sausage, sliced

1 tablespoon minced garlic

1 tablespoon paprika

1 teaspoon cumin

½ teaspoon cayenne pepper

3½ cups chicken stock or broth

1½ cups long-grain white rice, uncooked

2 tomatoes, chopped

1 teaspoon salt

½ teaspoon pepper

1 pound shrimp, peeled and deveined

1 MELT butter in a skillet over medium-high heat. Add celery, onion, bell pepper, sausage, garlic, paprika, cumin, and cayenne pepper and sauté 5 minutes. (You can also do this right in the crock of many modern slow cookers by using the cooker's browning function.)

2 REMOVE from heat and stir in chicken broth before transferring to a slow cooker.

3 ADD rice, tomatoes, salt, and pepper to the cooker.

4 SET the cooker to HIGH, cover, and let cook 2 hours, stirring in shrimp in the last 15 minutes.

Helpful Hint

You can substitute 1 (14½-ounce) can of diced tomatoes (drained) for the 2 fresh tomatoes.

Pizza Pasta

Pizzeria Flavors in a Slow Cooker Casserole

This casserole recipe is a family favorite that can please even the pickiest in the bunch. While I prefer using ground Italian sausage, ground meat can be used if anyone is not a fan of fennel seeds.

Shopping List

16 ounces rotini pasta

2 teaspoons olive oil

1 pound ground Italian sausage

1 (24-ounce) jar pasta sauce

1 (12-ounce) jar pizza sauce

4 ounces sliced turkey pepperoni

½ cup diced red onion

½ cup diced green bell pepper

1 teaspoon Italian seasoning

¼ teaspoon salt

½ cup grated Parmesan cheese

1 cup shredded mozzarella cheese

1 BOIL rotini about 8 minutes, draining while still very al dente.

2 MEANWHILE, place olive oil in a large skillet over medium-high heat. Add ground sausage, and cook until brown, about 5 minutes. Drain well. (You can also do this right in the crock of many modern slow cookers by using the cooker's browning function.)

3 TRANSFER the drained macaroni to a slow cooker sprayed with nonstick cooking spray. Top with browned sausage and all remaining ingredients, except mozzarella cheese. Stir to combine.

4 SET the cooker to LOW, cover, and let cook 2 hours.

5 TOP with mozzarella cheese, and continue cooking uncovered an additional 30 minutes before serving.

Helpful Tip

I use turkey pepperoni in this recipe because regular pepperoni releases too much grease as it cooks.

Slow Cooker Mac and Cheese

As Close to Oven-Baked As You Can Get Without an Oven

Those who know me know how much I like my mac and cheese, so when it came time to develop recipes for the slow cooker, how could I forget it? I tested and tweaked this recipe nearly a dozen times to get things just right, though I will admit that those last few tests were just because I wanted more!

Shopping List

16 ounces elbow macaroni

2 (12-ounce) cans evaporated milk

1 large egg

8 ounces processed cheese (such as Velveeta), chopped

2 cups shredded sharp Cheddar cheese

2 tablespoons butter or margarine, melted

½ teaspoon ground mustard

¼ teaspoon paprika

½ teaspoon salt

1 BOIL elbow macaroni 6–8 minutes, draining while still very al dente.

2 TRANSFER the drained macaroni to a slow cooker sprayed with nonstick cooking spray.

3 WHISK together evaporated milk and egg and pour over the macaroni in the cooker.

4 COVER with remaining ingredients, folding to combine.

5 SET the cooker to LOW, cover, and let cook 2 hours, stirring halfway through.

Helpful Tip

If you like crispy edges on your macaroni and cheese, use a spatula to pull the macaroni away from the edge of the cooker to check on how brown it is getting, and continue cooking until your liking.

Turkey Sausage Strata

A Brunch-Time Bread Pudding

This strata recipe is best when assembled in the crock of a slow cooker the night before, covered, and refrigerated overnight. In the morning you can start the cooking process to have it ready just in time for brunch.

Shopping List

1 tablespoon butter or margarine

1 pound ground turkey sausage

1 yellow onion, diced

¼ cup diced red bell pepper

6 cups cubed French bread, divided

1 (8-ounce) brick cream cheese, sliced

8 large eggs

1 (12-ounce) can evaporated milk

¼ teaspoon onion powder

1 teaspoon salt

¼ teaspoon pepper

Helpful Hint

The ground turkey sausage that is best in this recipe is ground breakfast sausage sold in a tube. Ground pork sausage will also work, as long as you drain it well.

1 SPRAY a slow cooker with nonstick cooking spray.

2 PLACE butter in a skillet over high heat, until sizzling. Add ground turkey sausage, onion, and bell pepper, and sauté 5 minutes, just until turkey is browned. Drain well. (You can also do this right in the crock of many modern slow cookers by using the cooker's browning function.)

3 PLACE ½ of the cubed bread at the bottom of a slow cooker.

4 TOP bread with the turkey sausage mixture and then evenly disperse the sliced cream cheese. Then top that with the remaining cubed bread.

5 WHISK together eggs, evaporated milk, onion powder, salt, and pepper. Pour over top of all in slow cooker.

6 SET the cooker to LOW, cover, and let cook 5 hours, or until eggs have set all the way through.

Sweet Potato Casserole

A Great Way to Save Precious Holiday Oven Real Estate

What would the holidays be without a slow cooker? While the turkey is roasting in the oven, this most-requested casserole can take its sweet time cooking away from the chaos of the rest of the big meal cooking on the stove.

Shopping List

2 pounds sweet potatoes

¼ cup dark brown sugar

¼ cup chopped pecans

2 tablespoons butter or margarine, melted

½ teaspoon vanilla extract

¾ teaspoon pumpkin pie spice

¼ teaspoon salt

1 cup miniature marshmallows

1 PEEL and chop sweet potatoes into chunks no more than 1 inch thick.

2 PLACE chopped potatoes and all remaining ingredients, except marshmallows, into a slow cooker. Fold together to evenly coat with spices.

3 SET the cooker to LOW, cover, and let cook 5 hours.

4 TOP with marshmallows, re-cover, and let cook an additional 15–30 minutes, or until marshmallows are warm and gooey. Serve using a slotted spoon.

Cut the Cost

If you do not have any pumpkin pie spice on hand, you can easily substitute ½ teaspoon of ground cinnamon and a small pinch of nutmeg.

Slow Cooker Lasagna

Slow Cooked for Flavors That Really Meld

Once you get past the fact that it's nearly impossible to cut a perfect slice of lasagna out of a slow cooker, you learn to appreciate just how simple, delicious, and convenient this recipe really is.

Shopping List

1 tablespoon olive oil

1 yellow onion, diced

1 pound lean ground beef

Salt and pepper to taste

1 (24-ounce) jar chunky spaghetti sauce

2 pounds whole-milk ricotta cheese

2 large eggs

⅓ cup grated Parmesan cheese

2 teaspoons minced garlic

1 teaspoon Italian seasoning

2 cups shredded mozzarella cheese, divided

8 ounces no-boil lasagna noodles

Helpful Hint

Cooking this in an oval slow cooker will make for easier serving, but a round cooker works fine. This just isn't the type of lasagna you can slice into perfect squares!

1 HEAT olive oil in a large skillet over high heat. Add onion, ground beef, and a pinch of salt and pepper. Sauté until meat is browned.

2 STIR spaghetti sauce into the ground beef mixture, and remove from heat.

3 IN a large mixing bowl, use a fork to whisk together ricotta cheese, eggs, Parmesan cheese, garlic, Italian seasoning, a pinch of salt and pepper, and 1 cup mozzarella cheese.

4 SPOON ⅕ of the beef and sauce mixture into the bottom of a slow cooker, and then cover with a full layer of lasagna noodles, breaking them to fit, if necessary.

5 COVER the noodles with a layer of ⅓ of the cheese mixture. Cover the cheese mixture with another layer of ⅕ of the sauce, then another layer of noodles. Repeat for 2 more layers, ending with only noodles topped with the final layer of sauce.

6 SET the cooker to LOW, cover, and let cook 5 hours, or until noodles are tender.

7 TOP with remaining cup of mozzarella cheese and cover 15 minutes to melt before serving.

Chicken Carbonara Pasta

Penne Pasta with Bacon, Egg, Peas, and Parmesan Cheese

Traditional Italian Carbonara is made with pancetta, Pecorino Romano cheese, and a whole lot of egg, but the American version is more like Alfredo sauce with peas. My version is the perfect marriage of the two, with a sauce that is still creamy like Alfredo, but incorporates an egg for added flavor.

Shopping List

6 strips thick-cut bacon, chopped

1¼ pounds boneless, skinless chicken breasts, sliced

1 red onion, diced

2 teaspoons minced garlic

2 (12-ounce) cans evaporated milk

1 large egg

1 tablespoon all-purpose flour

1 teaspoon salt

½ teaspoon pepper

8 ounces penne pasta

1 cup frozen peas

1 cup grated Parmesan cheese

Make It Better

This is typically made with diced pancetta (Italian bacon). It is sometimes sold in a refrigerated case in the deli and definitely worth substituting in place of the regular bacon.

1 PLACE bacon in a skillet over medium-high heat, and cook until crisp. Remove cooked bacon and reserve. (You can also do this right in the crock of many modern slow cookers by using the cooker's browning function.)

2 ADD sliced chicken to the bacon grease in the skillet, and brown on both sides, about 5 minutes.

3 TRANSFER browned chicken and cooked bacon to a slow cooker and cover with red onion and garlic.

4 WHISK together evaporated milk, egg, flour, salt, and pepper and pour into cooker.

5 SET the cooker to LOW, cover, and let cook 5 hours.

6 COOK pasta until al dente and drain well.

7 STIR cooked pasta, frozen peas, and Parmesan cheese into cooker and cook an additional 20–30 minutes, just until peas are heated through.

Best Ever Enchilada Casserole

You're Going to Need a Bigger Fork

I have a habit of naming my favorite recipes "Best Ever" but I do it for a reason, because I've run out of other words to explain just how good something like this enchilada casserole is. With only a handful of non-pantry staples, I could have also named this Easiest Ever Enchilada Casserole, but that is far too many words starting with the letter E!

Shopping List

1 tablespoon olive oil

1 pound lean ground beef

1 red onion, diced

½ cup diced green bell pepper

1 teaspoon chili powder

½ teaspoon cumin

¾ teaspoon salt

1 (16-ounce) jar chunky salsa

1 (15-ounce) can black beans, drained

1 (4-ounce) can mild green chiles, drained

12 (6-inch) soft flour tortillas

2 cups shredded Mexican cheese blend

1 HEAT olive oil in a large skillet over high heat. Add ground beef, onion, bell pepper, chili powder, cumin, and salt. Sauté until meat is browned.

2 STIR salsa, black beans, and green chiles into the ground beef mixture, and remove from heat.

3 SPOON ⅕ of the beef and sauce mixture into the bottom of a slow cooker, and then cover with 3 overlapped tortillas.

4 COVER the tortillas with another ⅕ of the sauce mixture, and then ¼ of the cheese blend.

5 REPEAT with tortillas, then sauce, then cheese 3 more times, ending with cheese on top.

6 SET the cooker to LOW, cover, and let cook 6 hours before serving.

Helpful Hint

Adding 1 cup of frozen lima beans to the sauce in Step 2 is a nice way to add more nutrition to this casserole when serving as a complete meal.

Cajun Chicken Pasta

With Tomato, Bell Pepper, and Broccoli

This all-in-one pasta meal with chicken and vegetables packs the kick of Cajun spices in a creamy sauce. If using a Cajun seasoning with added salt, omit the additional salt in the recipe and add it to taste after cooking.

Shopping List

1 tablespoon butter or margarine

1¼ pounds boneless, skinless chicken breasts, sliced

1 green bell pepper, diced

1 tomato, diced

2 (12-ounce) cans evaporated milk

¼ cup all-purpose flour

2 teaspoons Cajun seasoning

¼ teaspoon garlic powder

¼ teaspoon onion powder

1 teaspoon salt

½ teaspoon pepper

8 ounces rotini pasta

2 cups frozen broccoli florets, thawed

4 green onions, sliced

1 PLACE butter in a skillet over medium-high heat, heating until sizzling. Add sliced chicken, and brown on both sides, about 5 minutes. (You can also do this right in the crock of many modern slow cookers by using the cooker's browning function.)

2 TRANSFER browned chicken to a slow cooker and cover with bell pepper and tomato.

3 WHISK together evaporated milk, flour, Cajun seasoning, garlic powder, onion powder, salt, and pepper, and pour into cooker.

4 SET the cooker to LOW, cover, and let cook 5 hours.

5 COOK pasta until al dente, and drain well.

6 STIR cooked pasta, thawed broccoli, and green onions into cooker, and cook an additional 30 minutes before serving.

Make It Better

Add 1 cup of diced Andouille or smoked sausage to this before slow cooking for even more Cajun flavors.

Broccoli Casserole

The Perfect Potluck Side Dish

This, my take on a classic casserole, uses fresh ingredients instead of canned condensed soup, and it definitely shows in the end result. Broccoli has never been so irresistible.

Shopping List

1 large bunch broccoli

½ cup chopped green onions

¼ cup chicken stock or broth

½ (8-ounce) brick cream cheese, cubed

1 cup shredded sharp Cheddar cheese

1 tablespoon butter or margarine

¼ teaspoon garlic powder

½ teaspoon salt

¼ teaspoon pepper

2 tablespoons all-purpose flour

½ cup crumbled Ritz Crackers

1 CHOP broccoli into small florets, discarding large stems.

2 PLACE chopped broccoli florets in a slow cooker sprayed with nonstick cooking spray.

3 COVER with remaining ingredients, except all-purpose flour and crumbled crackers, and fold together.

4 SET the cooker to LOW, cover, and let cook 1 hour.

5 WHISK the all-purpose flour into 2 table-spoons of water, and stir into the cooker until everything is well combined. Pat down with the back of a spoon. Cover and let cook 1 additional hour.

6 SERVE topped with crumbled crackers.

Helpful Tips

To ensure broccoli cooks all the way through, cut small florets that are about the size of a quarter. You can also make this with 32 ounces of frozen baby broccoli florets to save on prep time.

Beef

Slow Cooker Pot Roast

My Favorite Pot Roast Recipe, Reimagined for the Slow Cooker

Pot roast has become the king of slow cooker comfort foods for good reason: the slow rendering allows the natural fat to melt into the meat, leaving you with savory, tender meat that can't be beat.

Shopping List

1 (2- to 3-pound) beef chuck roast

3 tablespoons all-purpose flour

Salt and pepper to taste

2 tablespoons olive oil

1½ cups beef stock or broth

2 tablespoons balsamic vinegar

1 tablespoon minced garlic

1 teaspoon dry thyme

2 bay leaves

1 teaspoon salt

¼ teaspoon pepper

6 redskin potatoes, halved

1 yellow onion, cut into wedges

2 cups baby carrots

2 ribs celery, cut into 1-inch lengths

2 tablespoons cornstarch

3 tablespoons butter or margarine

Make It Better

Try stirring in ¼ cup of heavy cream or sour cream in the last step for a richer, creamier gravy.

1 SPRINKLE the chuck roast with flour that has been generously seasoned with salt and pepper.

2 PLACE olive oil in a skillet over high heat, until nearly smoking hot. Add floured beef, and brown on both sides, about 5 minutes. (You can also do this right in the crock of many modern slow cookers by using the cooker's browning function.)

3 REMOVE skillet from heat, and then deglaze the pan with the beef stock, scraping any browned bits from the bottom.

4 TRANSFER beef and all liquid from the skillet to a slow cooker and top with the vinegar, garlic, thyme, bay leaves, salt, and pepper, tossing all to combine.

5 PLACE the potatoes, onion, carrots, and celery on top. Set the cooker to LOW, cover, and let cook 7 hours.

6 WHISK cornstarch into 2 tablespoons of water and stir into the cooking liquid. Re-cover, set the cooker to HIGH, and let cook 1 additional hour or until meat is fork-tender.

7 TURN off heat, stir in butter, and serve roast smothered with the vegetables and gravy.

Barbecue Pulled Beef

For Amazing Sandwiches and Picnic Platters

This pulled beef in a homemade barbecue sauce is great on sandwiches or as an entrée with your favorite cookout side dishes. It also makes enough to fill at least 24 slider buns for appetizers, too!

Shopping List

1 (3- to 4-pound) boneless beef chuck roast

1 cup ketchup

⅓ cup root beer

½ cup dark brown sugar

⅓ cup red wine vinegar

3 tablespoons Dijon mustard

1 tablespoon Worcestershire sauce

2 teaspoons paprika

1½ teaspoons onion powder

½ teaspoon garlic powder

1 teaspoon salt

1 teaspoon pepper

1 PLACE chuck roast in a slow cooker.

2 WHISK together all remaining ingredients and pour over roast.

3 SET the cooker to LOW, cover, and let cook 8 hours, or until meat is fork-tender.

4 USING 2 forks, shred the beef into the sauce before serving on sandwiches or as an entrée alongside picnic sides.

Helpful Hint

Any beef roast will work with this recipe, but roasts thicker than 3 inches thick should be cut in half to get tender enough to shred in 8 hours.

Slow Cooker Meatloaf

With No Need to Worry About It Drying Out

Believe it or not, meatloaf cooked in a slow cooker is not only possible, but actually great. The slow cooking really locks in the moisture, while also allowing you to free up your day while dinner cooks.

Shopping List

2 pounds lean ground beef

½ cup Italian bread crumbs

¼ cup grated Parmesan cheese

½ cup finely minced yellow onion

¼ cup milk

1 large egg, beaten

2 teaspoons minced garlic

1 teaspoon Italian seasoning

1 teaspoon salt

½ teaspoon pepper

1 (12-ounce) bottle chili sauce

1 COMBINE all ingredients, except chili sauce.

2 USING your hands, form the mixture into a round or oval loaf, small enough to fit into your slow cooker without touching the sides.

3 POUR chili sauce into the crock of your slow cooker. Place the formed loaf over top.

4 SET the cooker to LOW, cover, and let cook 8 hours, or until a meat thermometer registers 165°.

5 LET rest 10 minutes before slicing and serving, topped with chili sauce from the cooker.

Make It Easier

Triple-fold a long strip of aluminum foil and place it into your slow cooker, making sure it hugs the walls of the cooker. Then place the meatloaf over this strip before cooking to use the foil as handles to easily remove the cooked loaf later.

French Dip Sandwiches

With a Simple and Flavorful au Jus

Making extra tender roast beef and au jus for the perfect French Dip Sandwiches is an easy task for the slow cooker, and my recipe couldn't make things any easier.

Shopping List

1 bottom round beef roast (about 4 pounds)

3 cups beef stock or broth

1 (1¼-ounce) packet onion soup mix

¾ teaspoon black pepper

Hoagie rolls and provolone cheese, to serve

1 PLACE roast in a slow cooker and cover with beef broth, onion soup mix, and pepper.

2 SET the cooker to LOW, cover, and let cook 8–10 hours, or until meat is fork-tender.

3 TRANSFER roast to a cutting board and let rest under aluminum foil at least 10 minutes before carving into thin slices.

4 PLACE sliced beef on hoagie rolls and top with provolone cheese before dipping the sandwiches in the hot au jus in the cooker and serving.

Helpful Hint

This recipe is also a very simple roast beef recipe that you can serve carved up as an entrée. Whisk 2 tablespoons of cornstarch into 2 tablespoons of cold water and add to the au jus, bringing it to a boil to create a simple gravy. Remove gravy from heat and stir in 4 tablespoons of butter to make it even better.

"Stuffed" Butternut Squash

Tender and Sweet Squash with Spiced Ground Beef

I love to stuff squash or miniature pumpkins with spiced ground beef in the fall and roast them, though the ground beef on top sometimes has a tendency to dry out. This take on that concept uses cubed squash instead of stuffing the whole thing, but cooking in a covered slow cooker ensures the beef does not dry out.

Shopping List

4 cups cubed butternut squash

2 teaspoons vegetable oil

1¼ pounds lean ground beef

1 yellow onion, diced

2 tablespoons butter or margarine

1 teaspoon cider vinegar

½ teaspoon onion powder

¼ teaspoon ground cinnamon

¼ teaspoon ground allspice

¾ teaspoon salt

¼ teaspoon pepper

1 PLACE cubed butternut squash at the bottom of a slow cooker.

2 PLACE vegetable oil in a large skillet over medium-high heat. Add ground beef, and brown well, about 5 minutes. (You can also do this right in the crock of many modern slow cookers by using the cooker's browning function.)

3 WHEN meat is almost browned, drain off any excess fat, return to heat, and add onion, cooking just until they sweat.

4 STIR remaining ingredients into the meat mixture and then pour over the squash in the slow cooker.

5 SET the cooker to LOW, cover, and let cook 6 hours before serving.

Helpful Hint

Cubed butternut squash is often sold in the freezer aisle to make for much easier prep work.

Beef Roast with Horseradish Gravy

With Creamy Gravy That Packs a Real Kick

When ordering roast beef from a restaurant, I'm always sure to request a side of horseradish sauce as it pairs so well. And so, it made perfect sense to incorporate the essence of that powerful condiment directly into the sauce for this roast.

Shopping List

1 (3-pound) boneless beef roast

Salt and pepper to taste

Garlic powder to taste

2 tablespoons olive oil

1½ cups beef stock or broth

3 tablespoons prepared horseradish

1 tablespoon minced garlic

1 teaspoon dried thyme

1 teaspoon sugar

1 teaspoon salt

¼ teaspoon pepper

1 yellow onion, cut into wedges

6 redskin potatoes, halved

1 tablespoon cornstarch

3 tablespoons butter or margarine

Helpful Tip

The "prepared horseradish" called for in this recipe is usually found refrigerated in the produce section.

1 GENEROUSLY season the roast with salt, pepper, and garlic powder.

2 PLACE olive oil in a skillet over high heat, until nearly smoking hot. Add seasoned roast, and brown on all sides, about 5 minutes. (You can also do this right in the crock of many modern slow cookers by using the cooker's browning function.)

3 REMOVE skillet from heat and deglaze the pan with the beef stock, scraping any browned bits from the bottom.

4 TRANSFER roast and all liquid from the skillet to a slow cooker and top with remaining ingredients, except cornstarch and butter.

5 SET the cooker to LOW, cover, and let cook 7 hours.

6 WHISK cornstarch into 2 tablespoons of water and stir into the cooking liquid. Re-cover, set the cooker to HIGH, and let cook 1 additional hour, or until meat is fork-tender.

7 TURN off heat, stir in the butter, and serve roast thinly sliced alongside potatoes. Smother all in horseradish gravy.

Stuffed Peppers

A One-Bowl Meal Where You Can Actually Eat the Bowl

Stuffed peppers are one of my favorite things to prepare when entertaining, as the presentation is entertaining in itself. If using an oval slow cooker, this recipe can be multiplied by 1½-times to serve six people.

Shopping List

4 medium bell peppers, any color

1 pound extra lean ground beef

¼ cup minced onion

⅔ cup instant rice, uncooked

2 tablespoons milk

1 tablespoon chopped parsley

¾ teaspoon Italian seasoning

½ teaspoon garlic powder

¼ teaspoon onion powder

¾ teaspoon salt

½ teaspoon pepper

1 (25-ounce) jar prepared spaghetti sauce

1 CUT tops off bell peppers and scrape out seeds to create bell pepper cups.

2 COMBINE the remaining ingredients, except spaghetti sauce, to create the filling.

3 PACK an equal amount of the filling into each bell pepper cup and then place upright in a slow cooker. Cover all with spaghetti sauce.

4 SET the cooker to LOW, cover, and let cook 6 hours, or until ground beef is cooked throughout. Serve each stuffed pepper smothered in sauce.

Make It Better

You can use 1¼ cups cooked "ready" wild rice (sold in a microwavable pouch) in place of the instant rice for something with more whole grains.

Plum Good Short Ribs

A Restaurant-Quality Dish from Your Slow Cooker

Short ribs pair very well with fruit, especially the fresh plums used in this dish. Though it may sound strange at first, the end result is quite savory and delicious. If plums are not available though, try this with fresh figs—it's just as good!

Shopping List

1 tablespoon olive oil

3–4 pounds bone-in short ribs, trimmed of excess fat

1 yellow onion, diced

½ cup beef stock or broth

4 plums, halved and pitted

½ cup orange juice

1 tablespoon red wine vinegar

¼ cup dark brown sugar

2 tablespoons all-purpose flour

½ teaspoon salt

¼ teaspoon pepper

2 bay leaves

3 tablespoons butter or margarine

Helpful Tip

If you cannot find beef short ribs at your local grocery store, you can also prepare this with 3–4 pounds of country-style pork ribs.

1 PLACE olive oil in a skillet over high heat, until nearly smoking hot. Add short ribs, and brown on both sides, about 5 minutes. (You can also do this right in the crock of many modern slow cookers by using the cooker's browning function.)

2 ADD yellow onion to the skillet and then deglaze the pan with the beef stock, scraping any browned bits from the bottom.

3 TRANSFER short ribs, onion, and all liquid from the skillet to a slow cooker and top with plums.

4 WHISK together orange juice, red wine vinegar, brown sugar, flour, salt, and pepper, and pour over everything in the slow cooker.

5 ADD bay leaves, set the cooker to LOW, cover, and let cook 8 hours, or until meat is fork-tender.

6 STIR butter or margarine into the sauce before serving over short ribs.

Traditional Beef Stroganoff

with Chunks of Tender Beef in a Creamy Sauce

First originating in 1860's Russia, Beef Stroganoff has evolved a bit over the centuries to include—much like this version does—sour cream and fresh vegetables mixed right into the sauce.

Shopping List

1 (2- to 3-pound) beef chuck roast, cut into 1-inch cubes

3 tablespoons all-purpose flour

Salt and pepper to taste

3 tablespoons olive oil

1 cup beef stock or broth

1 white onion, chopped

2 stalks celery, chopped

8 ounces button mushrooms, stems removed

½ teaspoon garlic powder

½ teaspoon onion powder

¼ teaspoon allspice

1½ cups reduced-fat sour cream

Egg noodles, cooked, to serve

1 Toss the beef cubes in flour that has been generously seasoned with salt and pepper.

2 Place olive oil in a skillet over high heat, until almost smoking hot. Add floured beef, and brown on all sides, about 5 minutes. (You can also do this right in the crock of many modern slow cookers by using the cooker's browning function.)

3 Remove skillet from heat and deglaze the pan with the beef stock, scraping any browned bits from the bottom.

4 Transfer beef cubes and all liquid from the skillet to a slow cooker, and top with remaining ingredients, except sour cream and egg noodles.

5 Set the cooker to LOW, cover, and let cook 8 hours.

6 Turn off heat, stir in sour cream, and add salt and pepper to taste. Serve over buttered egg noodles.

Helpful Tip

Egg noodles cook fast and are easily boiled on the stove just minutes before you are ready to serve the stroganoff.

Beef Burgundy

Serve over Buttered Noodles or Toast Points

The aromatic flavors in this iconic stewed dish are pure French cooking at its best. While we like to eat this dish over noodles, it's traditionally served over toast!

Shopping List

1 (2- to 3-pound) beef chuck roast, cut into 1-inch cubes

3 tablespoons all-purpose flour

Salt and pepper to taste

2 tablespoons olive oil

6 slices bacon, chopped

1½ cups beef stock or broth

1 white onion, cut into wedges

2 cups baby carrots

8 ounces button mushrooms

1½ cups Burgundy or dry red wine

2 tablespoons tomato paste

1 tablespoon minced garlic

1 teaspoon dried thyme

2 bay leaves

1 teaspoon salt

¼ teaspoon pepper

1 tablespoon cornstarch

3 tablespoons butter or margarine

2 tablespoons chopped parsley

Make It Different

The red wine in this recipe can be replaced with 2 tablespoons balsamic vinegar, and 1 cup additional beef broth.

1 Toss the beef cubes in flour that has been generously seasoned with salt and pepper.

2 PLACE olive oil and bacon in a skillet over high heat, and cook until bacon is almost crisp. Remove cooked bacon with a slotted spoon and reserve.

3 ADD floured beef, and brown on both sides, about 5 minutes. (You can also do this right in the crock of many modern slow cookers by using the cooker's browning function.)

4 REMOVE skillet from heat and deglaze the pan with the beef stock, scraping any browned bits from the bottom.

5 TRANSFER beef cubes and all liquid from the skillet to a slow cooker, and top with the cooked bacon.

6 ADD onion, carrots, mushrooms, wine, tomato paste, garlic, thyme, bay leaves, salt, and pepper. Set the cooker to LOW, cover, and let cook 7 hours.

7 WHISK the cornstarch into 1 tablespoon of water and stir into the cooking liquid. Re-cover, set the cooker to HIGH, and let cook 1 additional hour, or until meat is fork-tender.

8 TURN off heat, stir in butter and parsley, and serve.

Brown Sugar Brisket

In a Sweet and Smoky Sauce

Chili sauce (sold in bottles near the ketchup), dark brown sugar, and balsamic vinegar make a dark and rich barbecue-style sauce that perfectly coats the brisket in this recipe. Liquid smoke adds the smokiness you'd associate with a slow-smoked brisket.

Shopping List

1 (2- to 2½-pound) beef brisket

2 teaspoons paprika

½ teaspoon onion powder

¼ teaspoon garlic powder

1 teaspoon salt

½ teaspoon pepper

1 red onion, diced

1 cup chili sauce

2 tablespoons yellow mustard

3 tablespoons dark brown sugar

2 tablespoons balsamic vinegar

½ teaspoon liquid smoke

1 PLACE brisket in a slow cooker and sprinkle with paprika, onion powder, garlic powder, salt, and pepper. Lightly press the spices into the top of the brisket.

2 TOP the brisket with the diced onion, then remaining ingredients.

3 SET the cooker to LOW, cover, and let cook 8–10 hours, or until meat is fork-tender.

4 TRANSFER brisket to a cutting board and let rest under aluminum foil at least 5 minutes before carving into thin slices. Serve topped with sauce from the slow cooker.

Make It Better

For a thicker sauce, whisk 2 tablespoons cornstarch into 2 tablespoons water, and stir into the slow cooker in the last 30 minutes of the cook time. Cover and switch the cooker to HIGH for the last 30 minutes.

Kicked Up Corned Beef

With Mustard and Stout au Jus

Corned beef has always been a go-to choice for slow cookers, as it's a tough cut of meat that needs slow and steady cooking no matter how you prepare it. The rich flavor of the dark ale contrasts with the sweetness of the brown sugar perfectly.

Shopping List

1 (3- to 4-pound) corned beef brisket

24 ounces stout or dark ale (Guinness recommended)

1 cup water

3 tablespoons pickling spice (put inside a tea ball for a cleaner broth)

2 tablespoons whole-grain mustard

3 tablespoons dark brown sugar

2 large white onions, cut into wedges

4 stalks celery, cut into 3-inch lengths

6 redskin potatoes, halved

1 PLACE brisket in a slow cooker and cover with ale, water, pickling spice, mustard, and brown sugar.

2 TOP brisket with onions, celery, and potatoes.

3 SET the cooker to LOW, cover, and let cook 8–10 hours, or until meat is fork-tender.

4 TRANSFER brisket to a cutting board, and let rest under aluminum foil at least 10 minutes before carving against the grain into thin slices. Serve hot, topped with juices and vegetables from the slow cooker.

Make It Yours

Add 1 tablespoon cider vinegar, 1 cup apple juice, and 1 cup additional water in place of the stout in this recipe.

Beef Paprikash

Made with Sweet Hungarian Paprika

This traditional Hungarian dish is best described as fragrant, full of spice, and perfectly balanced by a creamy finish. Hungarian "sweet" paprika is a must-have that is now available at most grocery stores.

Shopping List

1 (2- to 3-pound) sirloin roast, cut into 1-inch cubes

½ cup all-purpose flour

Salt and pepper to taste

2 tablespoons olive oil

1½ cups beef stock or broth

3 tablespoons sweet paprika

1 teaspoon dried thyme

1 teaspoon dried marjoram

2 bay leaves

2 red bell peppers, seeded and chopped large

1 (14½-ounce) can diced tomatoes, undrained

1 teaspoon salt

¼ teaspoon pepper

1½ cups reduced-fat sour cream

White rice, cooked, to serve

1 Toss the beef cubes in flour that has been generously seasoned with salt and pepper.

2 PLACE olive oil in a skillet over high heat, until almost smoking hot. Add floured beef, and brown on all sides, about 5 minutes. (You can also do this right in the crock of many modern slow cookers by using the cooker's browning function.)

3 REMOVE skillet from heat, and deglaze the pan with the beef stock, scraping any browned bits from the bottom.

4 TRANSFER beef cubes and all liquid from the skillet to a slow cooker, and top with remaining ingredients, except sour cream and rice.

5 SET the cooker to LOW, cover, and let cook 8 hours.

6 TURN off heat, stir in sour cream, and serve over rice.

Make It Memorable

Although rice is great for this recipe, traditionally this is served over spaetzel, now available at most grocery stores.

Cottage Pie

A Hearty Meal That Is Almost Too Easy to Make

Most of us use a slow cooker to make our lives a little easier, and I will admit that I definitely take shortcuts from time to time. Though I am not a fan of using premade foods if I can avoid it, I've found that the refrigerated mashed potatoes sold in grocery stores now are pretty darn good, and far easier than mashing them from scratch when you are looking to make a simple family meal like this one.

Shopping List

1 tablespoon vegetable oil

1 yellow onion, diced

1 pound lean ground beef

1 beef bouillon cube, or 1 teaspoon beef base

¾ cup beef stock or broth

1 teaspoon Worcestershire sauce

¼ teaspoon pepper

1 cup frozen corn kernels

1 cup frozen peas

1 cup shredded sharp Cheddar cheese

1 (24-ounce) package prepared mashed potatoes

1 pinch paprika

1 Heat vegetable oil in a large skillet over high heat. Add onion and ground beef, and sauté until meat is browned.

2 Stir beef bouillon, beef stock, Worcestershire sauce, and pepper into the ground beef, just until bouillon cube has melted.

3 Transfer the ground beef mixture to a slow cooker and stir in corn and peas.

4 Top with the shredded Cheddar cheese, then spread mashed potatoes evenly over top of all. Sprinkle top with a pinch of paprika.

5 Set the cooker to LOW, cover, and let cook 5½ hours.

6 Set the cooker to HIGH, uncover, and cook 30 additional minutes to create a crust on the top of the potatoes before serving.

Helpful Hint

The prepared mashed potatoes this recipe calls for are sold as ready-made side dishes in the refrigerated section of the grocery store, but you can also use 3 cups of homemade mashed potatoes (if you have the time or leftovers).

Spanish Beef and Rice

A New Comfort Food Classic

One-pot meals with ground beef are a staple in many households, including my own. Quite simply, it's an inexpensive way to feed a whole lot of mouths. This recipe spices things up a bit, but don't worry, the heat isn't too much for kids.

Shopping List

1 tablespoon olive oil

2 pounds ground sirloin

1 large yellow onion, chopped

1 (28-ounce) can diced tomatoes, undrained

1 (16-ounce) jar chunky salsa

2 green bell peppers, seeded and chopped

1 cup long-grain rice

1 cup chicken stock or broth

2 tablespoons Worcestershire sauce

2 teaspoons minced garlic

2 tablespoons chili powder

1½ teaspoons cumin

1¼ teaspoons salt

½ teaspoon pepper

1 PLACE olive oil and ground sirloin in a large skillet over medium-high heat, browning well, about 5 minutes. (You can also do this right in the crock of many modern slow cookers by using the cooker's browning function.)

2 WHEN meat is almost browned, drain off any excess fat, return to heat, and add onions, just until they sweat.

3 TRANSFER beef and onions to a slow cooker and cover with remaining ingredients, stirring to combine.

4 SET the cooker to LOW, cover, and let cook 8 hours, or until rice is tender. Serve as is, or topped with shredded cheese and sour cream, if desired.

Make It Different

Any ground meat can be used in place of the sirloin in this recipe—feel free to buy whatever happens to be on sale!

Poultry

Honey Sesame Chicken

Asian-Inspired Chicken and a Sweet and Savory Sauce

This is just one of those entrées that you can't help but love, especially when served over white or fried rice. Or try serving alongside a homemade lo-mein by quickly stir-frying cooked linguine with a few splashes of soy sauce and two tablespoons of sesame oil.

Shopping List

2 pounds boneless, skinless chicken breasts or thighs

½ cup chopped scallions

3 tablespoons honey

2 tablespoons soy sauce

1 tablespoon sesame oil

1 tablespoon butter or margarine

Toasted sesame seeds, for garnish

1 PLACE chicken in a lightly greased skillet over high heat, and brown on both sides, about 5 minutes. (You can also do this right in the crock of many modern slow cookers by using the cooker's browning function.)

2 PLACE browned chicken in a slow cooker and cover with remaining ingredients, tossing to combine.

3 SET the cooker to LOW, cover, and let cook 5–6 hours, or until meat is tender and you are ready to serve.

4 TOP with toasted sesame seeds before serving.

Toasting Sesame Seeds

To toast sesame seeds, place 1–2 tablespoons of sesame seeds in a dry skillet over medium-high heat and shake the pan to keep them moving until seeds are fragrant and lightly browned.

Chicken and Biscuit "Pot Pie"

Not Your Typical Pot Pie

Making chicken pot pie in a slow cooker with a true crust simply isn't possible, yet slow cookers are the perfect way to cook a pot pie filling with truly tender chicken. I find that topping the filling with freshly baked biscuits gives you all the buttery, flaky goodness you want from a pot pie crust, but with far less work.

Shopping List

1¼ pounds boneless, skinless chicken breasts, cubed

Salt and pepper to taste

2 tablespoons butter or margarine

3 cups chopped potatoes

1 yellow onion, diced

3 (12-ounce) cans evaporated milk

1 teaspoon chicken base, or 1 chicken bouillon cube

1 teaspoon dried thyme

¼ teaspoon poultry seasoning

1 teaspoon salt

½ teaspoon pepper

1 (10-ounce) package frozen peas and carrots

3 tablespoons cornstarch

12 frozen or canned biscuits

¼ cup grated Parmesan cheese

1 GENEROUSLY season the cubed chicken with salt and pepper.

2 PLACE butter in a skillet over medium-high heat, until sizzling. Add seasoned chicken, and brown on both sides, about 5 minutes. (You can also do this right in the crock of many modern slow cookers by using the cooker's browning function.)

3 TRANSFER chicken to a slow cooker and top with potatoes, onion, evaporated milk, chicken base, thyme, poultry seasoning, salt, and pepper. Stir to combine.

4 SET the cooker to LOW, cover, and let cook 6 hours.

5 SET cooker to HIGH; whisk cornstarch into 3 tablespoons of water, and stir into the chowder. Add frozen peas and carrots, re-cover, and let cook 1 additional hour.

6 MEANWHILE bake biscuits according to package directions.

7 STIR Parmesan cheese into the chicken mixture before serving in bowls topped with 2 biscuits each.

Make It Different

Instead of topping with the biscuits, you can break 6 under-baked biscuits into pieces and stir into the dish to make a quick chicken and dumplings.

Chicken Cordon Bleu

With an Herbed Cheese Sauce

My take on Chicken Cordon Bleu uses only a few ingredients without resorting to canned soup to create the sauce. Instead, I make a creamy, cheesy sauce from herbed cream cheese, which I'd take over condensed soup any day! Though this isn't breaded like a typical Cordon Bleu, all the flavors are there and—using a slow cooker—the results are guaranteed to be tender.

Shopping List

4 boneless, skinless chicken breasts

Salt and pepper to taste

4 slices deli ham

4 slices Swiss cheese

½ teaspoon dried thyme

⅓ cup chicken stock or broth

4 ounces herbed cream cheese

Make It Different

For a more kid-friendly version of Chicken Cordon Bleu, Cheddar cheese can be used in place of the Swiss cheese and thyme can be reduced by half (for a less herbed flavor). One cup cubed Velveeta cheese can be used in place of the cream cheese for an extra-cheesy sauce.

1 LAY chicken breasts between 2 plastic wrap sheets, and use a meat mallet or rolling pin to pound down until about ⅓ inch thick.

2 GENEROUSLY season both sides of the flattened chicken with salt and pepper.

3 PLACE a slice of ham and then a slice of cheese into each of the chicken breasts before rolling each breast up tight.

4 PLACE each rolled chicken breast in a slow cooker, seam side down. Sprinkle all with thyme, and pour chicken stock into the bottom of the cooker.

5 SET the cooker to LOW, cover, and let cook 7 hours.

6 ADD herbed cream cheese to the cooking liquid and let cook 1 additional hour.

7 REMOVE rolled chicken breasts and thoroughly stir cream cheese into the cooking liquid to create a sauce. Serve chicken drizzled in sauce.

Chicken with Kalamata Olives

Simple Greek Flavors, Made Simply

The Mediterranean ingredients in this recipe are classics and classics for a reason. These chicken breasts, topped with kalamata olives, sliced red onion, and diced tomato, are about as simple, clean, and perfect as flavor combinations get.

Shopping List

4 boneless, skinless chicken breasts

Salt and pepper to taste

2 tablespoons olive oil

1 red onion, thinly sliced

1 large tomato, diced

⅔ cup pitted kalamata olives

½ cup chicken stock or broth

2 teaspoons minced garlic

1 teaspoon sugar

1 teaspoon lemon zest

1 teaspoon dried oregano

1 GENEROUSLY season the chicken breasts with salt and pepper.

2 PLACE olive oil in a skillet over high heat, until sizzling. Add seasoned chicken, and brown on both sides, about 5 minutes. (You can also do this right in the crock of many modern slow cookers by using the cooker's browning function.)

3 TRANSFER browned chicken to a slow cooker and top with onion, tomato, and olives.

4 COMBINE remaining ingredients and pour over top of all in the slow cooker.

5 SET the cooker to LOW, cover, and let cook 6 hours.

6 SERVE each chicken breast topped with olives, onion, and tomato from the cooker.

Make It a Meal

Add thick-sliced yellow squash and zucchini before cooking, and serve alongside couscous for a complete meal.

Roasted Red Pepper Chicken

With Goat Cheese Medallions

The complex flavors of roasted red peppers, soft goat cheese, and fresh rosemary pair so well together in this Italian-inspired dish, it will fool anyone invited over for dinner into thinking it took a lot of effort.

Shopping List

1 tablespoon olive oil

4–6 boneless, skinless chicken breasts

Salt and pepper to taste

½ cup Italian salad dressing

½ cup chicken stock or broth

1 tablespoon all-purpose flour

½ teaspoon chopped fresh rosemary

1 (12-ounce) jar roasted red peppers, drained

6 ounces goat cheese (log-shaped)

Make It Yours

Any soft or crumbled cheese works well in this recipe, though I especially like herbed goat cheese when I can find it. Fresh mozzarella cheese (usually sold in balls or submerged in water) is perfect if you are not a fan of stronger cheeses.

1 PLACE olive oil in a skillet over high heat, until nearly smoking hot. Generously season chicken with salt and pepper, and place in the skillet, browning on both sides, about 5 minutes. (You can also do this right in the crock of many modern slow cookers by using the cooker's browning function.)

2 TRANSFER browned chicken to a slow cooker.

3 WHISK together Italian dressing, chicken stock, flour, and rosemary and pour over the chicken in the slow cooker.

4 SET the cooker to LOW, cover, and let cook 5 hours.

5 ADD roasted red peppers to the cooker. Cover and let cook 1 additional hour.

6 SLICE goat cheese into thin medallions. Serve each chicken breast topped with 2–3 medallions of goat cheese, and then drizzle with red peppers and sauce from the cooker (this will warm the goat cheese as you serve).

Cashew Chicken

Super Simple Chinese Slow Cooking

My take on this Chinese take-out classic is not only easy, but filled with fresh, colorful vegetables. Serve over steamed white or brown rice for a full meal.

Shopping List

1¼ pounds boneless, skinless chicken breasts, sliced thick

1 small bunch broccoli, cut into small florets

1 red bell pepper, cut into strips

8 ounces sliced mushrooms

1 cup beef stock or broth

½ cup hoisin sauce

2 tablespoons soy sauce

2 tablespoons cornstarch

¼ teaspoon pepper

½ cup roasted cashews

1 PLACE chicken, broccoli, bell pepper, and mushrooms in a slow cooker.

2 WHISK together beef stock, hoisin sauce, soy sauce, cornstarch, and pepper. Pour over all in slow cooker and stir to combine.

3 SET the cooker to LOW, cover, and let cook 6 hours.

4 STIR in roasted cashews before serving.

Make It Better

Try adding a drained can of mandarin oranges along with the roasted cashews just before serving to make this dish even better.

Stuffed Turkey Meatloaf

With Cheddar Cheese and Zucchini

Ground turkey is notorious for being dry, especially lean ground turkey like called for in this recipe, but here the slow cooker locks in the moisture. Stuffing the meatloaf with whole cubes of Cheddar cheese and chunks of zucchini makes it even more moist.

Shopping List

2 pounds lean ground turkey

½ cup Italian bread crumbs

⅓ cup finely minced red onion

¼ cup milk

1 large egg, beaten

1 teaspoon Italian seasoning

½ teaspoon onion powder

1 teaspoon salt

½ teaspoon pepper

1 cup cubed Cheddar cheese

1 large zucchini, chopped

1 cup ketchup

1 tablespoon yellow mustard

1 WITH your hands, combine ground turkey, bread crumbs, onion, milk, egg, Italian seasoning, onion powder, salt, and pepper.

2 ADD the cubed cheese and chopped zucchini, and work it into the meat evenly throughout.

3 FORM the mixture into a round or oval loaf, small enough to fit into your slow cooker without touching the sides.

4 COMBINE ketchup and mustard in the crock of your slow cooker. Place the formed loaf over top.

5 SET the cooker to LOW, cover, and let cook 8 hours, or until a meat thermometer registers 170°.

6 LET rest 10 minutes before slicing and serving topped with sauce from the cooker.

Make It Easier

I recommend using lean ground turkey for this meatloaf. Regular ground turkey can be greasy, and extra lean or "ground turkey breast" can be too dry.

Jerk Chicken with Mango Salsa

Island Flavors with a Sweet and Savory Salsa

Spiced chicken served alongside vibrant mangoes will add a Caribbean shine to anyone's table. You will definitely find yourself nodding to the beat of this drum.

Shopping List

2 pounds chicken drums

1 cup all-purpose flour

Salt and pepper to taste

3 tablespoons olive oil

1 cup chicken stock or broth

3 tablespoons lime juice

2 tablespoons light brown sugar

1 tablespoon dried thyme

1 teaspoon ground ginger

1 teaspoon onion powder

½ teaspoon ground allspice

¼ teaspoon nutmeg

¼ teaspoon garlic powder

2 bay leaves

1 teaspoon salt

¼ teaspoon pepper

MANGO SALSA

2 ripe mangoes, diced

2 tablespoons lime juice

½ cup diced red bell pepper

¼ cup finely diced red onion

1 tablespoon chopped cilantro

1 COAT the chicken drums in flour that has been generously seasoned with salt and pepper.

2 PLACE olive oil in a skillet over high heat, until nearly smoking hot. Add floured chicken, and brown well on both sides, about 5 minutes. (You can also do this right in the crock of many modern slow cookers by using the cooker's browning function.)

3 REMOVE skillet from heat, and deglaze the pan with the chicken broth, scraping any browned bits from the bottom.

4 TRANSFER chicken and all liquid from the skillet to a slow cooker and top with all remaining chicken ingredients.

5 SET the cooker to LOW, cover, and let cook 8 hours.

6 WHILE the chicken cooks, make the MANGO SALSA by adding all salsa ingredients to a bowl and tossing to combine. Cover and refrigerate until needed. Serve alongside cooked chicken.

Helpful Hint

Mangoes aren't always available, so don't be afraid to mix it up by using other fruits like peaches or pineapple.

Apricot Chicken

Sweet, Tangy, and Absolutely Amazing

I love to include fresh fruit in savory dishes, especially those that are slow cooked, as over time, the flavors truly meld into something entirely different. Sage is added because its earthy flavor has just the right bitterness to offset the sweet apricots.

Shopping List

2 tablespoons butter or margarine

4–6 boneless, skinless chicken breasts

6 apricots, halved and pitted

½ cup diced red onion

⅓ cup apricot preserves

¼ cup chicken stock or broth

2 tablespoons red wine vinegar

2 tablespoons chopped sage leaves

½ teaspoon salt

¼ teaspoon pepper

1 ADD all ingredients to a slow cooker and toss to combine.

2 SET the cooker to LOW, cover, and let cook 5–6 hours, or until meat is cooked through and you are ready to serve.

3 FOR a thicker sauce, whisk 2 teaspoons cornstarch into 1 tablespoon water, and stir into the slow cooker in the last 30 minutes of the cook time. Cover and switch the cooker to HIGH for the last 30 minutes.

Make It Better

Browning the chicken in an oiled skillet over high heat (or using the browning function of many newer slow cookers) before slow cooking will add an additional level of flavor to this dish.

Chicken Thighs with Wild Rice

A Great Weeknight Meal

This homestyle dish is really two dishes in one—a chicken entrée with a side of wild rice—both seasoned with classic herbs, onion, and celery. Adding evaporated milk to the cooking liquid for the rice makes it creamier without adding too much fat.

Shopping List

2–3 pounds boneless, skinless chicken thighs

Salt and pepper to taste

3 tablespoons butter or margarine

1 yellow onion, diced

½ cup diced celery

2 cups wild rice, uncooked

1 (12-ounce) can evaporated milk

5 cups chicken stock or broth

1 teaspoon dried thyme

½ tcaspoon dried rosemary

½ teaspoon onion powder

¼ teaspoon garlic powder

½ teaspoon salt

½ teaspoon pepper

1 GENEROUSLY season the chicken thighs with salt and pepper and place in a slow cooker.

2 PLACE butter in a skillet over high heat, until sizzling. Add onion and celery, and sauté 5 minutes, just until onions begin to caramelize. (You can also do this right in the crock of many modern slow cookers by using the cooker's browning function.)

3 TRANSFER the cooked vegetables to the slow cooker and then top with remaining ingredients.

4 SET the cooker to LOW, cover, and let cook 8 hours.

Make It Better

I like to add 2 tablespoons of butter and 2 tablespoons of Parmesan cheese to the rice before serving to make it creamier.

Lemon and Artichoke Chicken

With Sun-Dried Tomatoes

If you were thinking chicken can get a bit boring, think again. Artichoke hearts, sun-dried tomatoes, and a touch of lemon juice can spruce things up, adding a sophisticated level of acidity and brightness even the pickiest of eaters will enjoy.

Shopping List

4–6 boneless, skinless chicken breasts

1 cup chicken stock or broth

2 tablespoons lemon juice

1 tablespoon all-purpose flour

1 teaspoon minced garlic

¾ teaspoon sugar

½ teaspoon salt

¼ teaspoon pepper

1 (12-ounce) jar marinated artichoke hearts, drained

⅓ cup julienned sun-dried tomatoes

3 tablespoons butter or margarine

1 LAY chicken breasts between 2 plastic wrap sheets, and use a meat mallet or rolling pin to pound down until about ½ inch thick. Place pounded chicken breasts into a slow cooker.

2 WHISK together chicken stock, lemon juice, flour, garlic, sugar, salt, and pepper and pour over the chicken in the slow cooker.

3 SET the cooker to LOW, cover, and let cook 5 hours.

4 ADD artichoke hearts and sun-dried tomatoes to the cooker and press down to fully submerge tomatoes. Cover and let cook 1 additional hour.

5 STIR butter or margarine into the sauce just before serving.

Make It Better

Browning the chicken in an oiled skillet over high heat (or using the browning function of many newer slow cookers) before slow cooking will add an additional level of flavor to this dish. If using browned chicken, cook time can be reduced to 4 hours.

Slow Cooker Turkey Breast

Tender Turkey Every Time

Like most meat cooked in a slow cooker, given enough time, a whole turkey breast cooks up so moist that you may wonder why you'll ever want to bake a turkey again. (An oval slow cooker is recommended unless you can find a small enough turkey breast for your four-quart cooker.)

Shopping List

1 (4- to 5-pound) bone-in turkey breast

2 cups chicken stock or broth

1 yellow onion, chopped

6 tablespoons butter or margarine

Juice of 1 lemon

1 teaspoon dried rosemary

1 teaspoon dried thyme

½ teaspoon poultry seasoning

1½ teaspoons salt

½ teaspoon pepper

1 PLACE the turkey, breast side down, in the crock of a slow cooker, and then pour chicken broth around it.

2 STUFF onion and butter into the cavity on the back of the turkey breast, placing any onion that will not fit into the surrounding broth. Drizzle lemon juice over top of the turkey and into the broth.

3 MIX and rub the remaining ingredients into the turkey, letting the excess fall into the broth.

4 SET the cooker to LOW, cover, and let cook 9 hours, or until a meat thermometer registers 170°.

5 REMOVE from slow cooker and let rest 15 minutes before discarding skin, carving, and serving drizzled with the juices from the cooker.

Make It Better

Use finely chopped leaves of one large sprig of thyme and one large sprig of rosemary in place of the dried herbs for even better flavor.

Chicken Parmesan

The Family Favorite, Cooked Tender Every Time

This is one of the easiest recipes for Chicken Parmesan that you could ever make. While it doesn't have the crispy crust of baked versions, slow cooking in the sauce ensures that the chicken is moist and tender.

Shopping List

4 boneless, skinless chicken breasts

1 cup all-purpose flour

Salt and pepper to taste

2 tablespoons olive oil

1 (25-ounce) jar prepared spaghetti sauce

1 teaspoon minced garlic

1 teaspoon Italian seasoning

¼ teaspoon salt

¼ cup grated Parmesan cheese

1½ cups shredded mozzarella cheese

Make It Better

Rather than melting the cheese in the cooker in Step 5, transfer the removable crock of your slow cooker to an oven preheated to 350° and bake 20–30 minutes to get the cheese nice and browned.

1 COAT the chicken breasts with flour that has been generously seasoned with salt and pepper.

2 PLACE olive oil in a skillet over high heat, until nearly smoking hot. Add floured chicken, and brown on both sides, about 5 minutes. (You can also do this right in the crock of many modern slow cookers by using the cooker's browning function.)

3 TRANSFER browned chicken to a slow cooker and top with spaghetti sauce, garlic, Italian seasoning, and salt.

4 SET the cooker to LOW, cover, and let cook 5 hours.

5 TOP all with Parmesan cheese and then mozzarella cheese. Continue cooking, uncovered, 1 hour, until cheese is melted and bubbly.

6 SERVE over your favorite pasta with sauce from the cooker.

Buffalo Pulled Chicken Sandwiches

Perfect Pulled Chicken with Few Ingredients

This pulled chicken has all the flavor (and heat) of buffalo wings, only delivered in a brand-new way. Serve it on kaiser rolls with your favorite fixings, though either crumbled bleu cheese or bleu cheese dressing is pretty much a prerequisite.

Shopping List

2 pounds boneless, skinless chicken breasts

Salt and pepper to taste

2 tablespoons Louisiana Hot Sauce

¼ cup chicken stock or broth

6 tablespoons butter or margarine

Kaiser rolls, lettuce, sliced tomato, and crumbled bleu cheese to serve

1 GENEROUSLY season the chicken breasts with salt and pepper and place in a slow cooker.

2 ADD hot sauce and chicken broth to the cooker.

3 SET the cooker to LOW, cover, and let cook 8 hours.

4 ADD butter and let melt into the sauce in the cooker.

5 USING a fork, shred cooked chicken into the sauce in the cooker.

6 SERVE shredded chicken on kaiser rolls with lettuce, tomato, and crumbled bleu cheese. To cool down the hot sauce further, you can serve with bleu cheese dressing spread on the buns in place of crumbled cheese.

Make It Memorable

To make these sandwiches really special, thinly slice celery using a kitchen slicer (mandolin) and let pickle in the pickling liquid from an empty jar of dill pickles as the chicken cooks. Then add the pickled celery to the finished sandwiches.

Chicken Cacciatore

An Easy Choice for a Family-Style Meal

Chicken so tender it falls off the bone, and practically dances in a rustic red sauce is what you get in this slow cooker staple that just about everyone has their own take on. My take is simple, yet still made from scratch.

Shopping List

4 chicken breasts, bone-in, with skin

1 cup flour, mixed with 2 pinches each: salt, pepper, and paprika

3 tablespoons olive oil

½ cup dry white wine

1 yellow onion, chopped large

1 green bell pepper, chopped large

1 (14½-ounce) can diced tomatoes

1 (8-ounce) can tomato sauce

3 tablespoons tomato paste

2 tablespoons minced garlic

1 tablespoon Italian seasoning

2 bay leaves

1 teaspoon salt

¼ teaspoon pepper

1 COAT the chicken breasts with seasoned flour.

2 PLACE olive oil in a skillet over high heat, until nearly smoking hot. Add floured chicken, and brown on both sides, about 5 minutes. (You can also do this right in the crock of many modern slow cookers by using the cooker's browning function.)

3 REMOVE skillet from heat, and then deglaze the pan with the wine, scraping any browned bits from the bottom.

4 TRANSFER chicken and all liquid from the skillet to a slow cooker and top with all remaining ingredients.

5 SET the cooker to LOW, cover, and let cook 8 hours. Serve over pasta with sauce from the cooker.

Helpful Hint

Chicken stock or broth and a splash of lemon juice can be substituted for the white wine in this recipe.

40 Clove Garlic Chicken

Garlic Cloves Roast Up Tender and Delicious

Surprisingly enough, forty cloves of garlic aren't overpowering, and actually mellow out when cooked down, taking on a buttery and nutty quality that makes this dish unique.

Shopping List

2 pounds chicken pieces, bone-in, with skin

½ cup all-purpose flour

Salt and pepper to taste

2 tablespoons olive oil

¼ cup dry white wine (may use 1 tablespoon cider vinegar)

½ cup chicken stock or broth

2 tablespoons butter or margarine

4 stalks celery, cut into 2-inch lengths

40 cloves garlic, peeled

1 teaspoon dried thyme

½ teaspoon dried rosemary

Make It Easier

Pre-peeled garlic cloves are usually sold in the refrigerated case of the produce department.

1 COAT the chicken pieces with flour that has been generously seasoned with salt and pepper.

2 PLACE olive oil in a skillet over high heat, until nearly smoking hot. Add floured chicken, and brown on both sides, about 5 minutes. (You can also do this right in the crock of many modern slow cookers by using the cooker's browning function.)

3 REMOVE skillet from heat and deglaze the pan with the wine and chicken broth, scraping any browned bits from the bottom.

4 TRANSFER chicken and all liquid from the skillet to a slow cooker and top with remaining ingredients.

5 SET cooker to LOW, cover, and let cook 8 hours.

6 TURN off heat, uncover, and salt and pepper chicken pieces to taste before serving.

Osso Buco Chicken Thighs

A Family-Friendly Approach to an Upscale Dish

Although many restaurants today have phased out veal from their menus for compassionate reasons, that doesn't mean they have forgone everyone's favorite veal recipes. Chicken replaces veal in this classic remake, and works wonderfully, as all the original flavors remain intact.

Shopping List

8 chicken thighs, bone-in

1 cup all-purpose flour

Salt and pepper to taste

3 tablespoons olive oil

1 cup dry red wine

½ cup chicken stock or broth

1 red onion, chopped

2 tablespoons minced garlic

2 carrots, cut into ¼-inch thick discs

2 stalks celery, chopped

1 (14½-ounce) can diced tomatoes, drained

1 (8-ounce) can tomato sauce

2 tablespoons tomato paste

2 teaspoons Italian seasoning

1 teaspoon salt

¼ teaspoon pepper

1 COAT chicken thighs with flour that has been generously seasoned with salt and pepper.

2 PLACE olive oil in a skillet over high heat, until nearly smoking hot. Add floured chicken, and brown on both sides, about 5 minutes. (You can also do this right in the crock of many modern slow cookers by using the cooker's browning function.)

3 REMOVE skillet from heat, and then deglaze the pan with the wine, scraping any browned bits from the bottom.

4 TRANSFER chicken and all liquid from the skillet to a slow cooker and top with all remaining ingredients.

5 SET the cooker to LOW, cover, and let cook 8 hours.

6 TURN off heat, and serve thighs smothered in the vegetables and sauce.

Make It a Meal

For a full meal, serve alongside gnocchi dumplings that have been boiled and then pan-fried in butter.

Chicken Veronique

Chicken with Green Grapes in a Tarragon Cream Sauce

Veronique simply means "to garnish with grapes," but this savory French dish is also known for its delicious tarragon cream sauce that perfectly balances the sweetness of the grapes.

Shopping List

4–6 boneless, skinless chicken breasts

Salt and pepper to taste

2 tablespoons butter or margarine

1 tablespoon vegetable oil

1 yellow onion, thinly sliced

1 cup chicken stock or broth

1 teaspoon minced garlic

1 teaspoon cider vinegar

¾ teaspoon dried tarragon

⅛ teaspoon ground nutmeg

1 tablespoon cornstarch

¼ cup half-and-half

2 cups green grapes, halved

1 GENEROUSLY season the chicken breasts with salt and pepper.

2 PLACE butter and olive oil in a skillet over high heat, until sizzling. Add seasoned chicken, and brown on both sides, about 5 minutes. (You can also do this right in the crock of many modern slow cookers by using the cooker's browning function.)

3 TRANSFER browned chicken to a slow cooker and top with onion, chicken stock, garlic, vinegar, tarragon, and nutmeg.

4 SET the cooker to LOW, cover, and let cook 5 hours.

5 WHISK cornstarch into half and half, and stir into the cooker. Add the grapes, re-cover, and continue cooking 1 hour, or until sauce is bubbling and thickened.

6 SEASON the sauce with salt and pepper to taste before serving.

Make It Better

Omitting the cider vinegar and substituting ½ cup of white wine in place of ½ cup of the chicken broth will make this a more traditional version of Chicken Veronique.

Coconut Curry Chicken

Far East Flavors Made at Home

The secret to a thick and rich curry sauce like the one in this dish is processing whole vegetables into the sauce before cooking. The flavors of the vegetables and spices combine and cook into something far more complex than the simple ingredients would have you think.

Shopping List

2 pound boneless, skinless chicken breasts, cubed

1½ cups coconut milk

1 yellow onion, quartered

1 green bell pepper, chopped

1 (6-ounce) can tomato paste

1 tablespoon curry powder

2 teaspoons minced garlic

½ teaspoon cumin

¼ teaspoon ground cinnamon

¼ teaspoon white pepper

⅛ teaspoon cayenne pepper

1¼ teaspoons salt

¼ teaspoon pepper

1 tablespoon cornstarch

1 PLACE cubed chicken in a slow cooker.

2 PLACE all remaining ingredients, except cornstarch, into a food processor and process until nearly entirely smooth.

3 POUR the processed mixture over the chicken in the slow cooker.

4 SET the cooker to LOW, cover, and let cook 5 hours.

5 WHISK cornstarch into 2 tablespoons of water and stir into the cooking liquid. Re-cover and let cook 1 additional hour, or until meat is fork-tender. Serve over basmati or regular white rice.

Helpful Hint

The spices in this recipe pack a punch. Serve topped with a dollop of plain yogurt to cool things down. Omit the cayenne pepper to cool things down further.

Pork

Country-Style Ribs

Prepped Quick and Easy

Country-style pork ribs are one of my favorite cuts of meat because you get a whole lot more meat on those bones. I've kept this recipe simple, using mostly pantry staples and your favorite prepared barbecue sauce—just don't skip on dry rubbing them before cooking—it makes all the difference!

Shopping List

3 pounds country-style pork ribs

1 teaspoon paprika

½ teaspoon onion powder

1 teaspoon salt

½ teaspoon pepper

1 tablespoon vegetable oil

1 yellow onion, diced

2 tablespoons cider vinegar

1 (18-ounce) bottle prepared bold barbecue sauce

1 tablespoon minced garlic

Helpful Tip

Depending on the water content of the pork, the sauce may thin out as it cooks. If the sauce is too watery before serving, simply ladle it into a saucepot, and rapidly simmer on the stove until thickened, about 15 minutes.

1   GENEROUSLY rub ribs with mixture of paprika, onion powder, salt, and pepper.

2   PLACE vegetable oil in a skillet over high heat, until nearly smoking hot. Add ribs, and brown on both sides, about 5 minutes. (You can also do this right in the crock of many modern slow cookers by using the cooker's browning function.)

3   ADD yellow onion to the skillet, remove from heat, and then deglaze the pan with the cider vinegar, scraping any browned bits from the bottom.

4   TRANSFER ribs, onions, and all liquid from the skillet to a slow cooker and top with barbecue sauce and minced garlic. Toss ribs to coat with sauce.

5   SET the cooker to LOW, cover, and let cook 8 hours, or until meat is fork-tender.

6   SERVE ribs drizzled in the sauce.

Teriyaki Pork Roast

Perfect Over White or Brown Rice

East meets West in this colorful pork dish, brightened by family-friendly teriyaki sauce. Toss in some baby carrots, a splash of orange juice, and snappy snow peas, and you've got a meal worthy of take-out.

Shopping List

1 (2- to 4-pound) pork roast

3 tablespoons all-purpose flour

Salt and pepper to taste

2 tablespoons vegetable oil

1 cup orange juice

1 cup teriyaki sauce

1 tablespoon sesame oil (optional)

1 yellow onion, cut into wedges

2 cups baby carrots

1 tablespoon minced garlic

1 teaspoon dried thyme

¼ teaspoon pepper

1½ tablespoons cornstarch

2 cups snow peas

2 tablespoons butter or margarine

Cut the Sodium

Use reduced-sodium teriyaki sauce to significantly cut the sodium in this recipe.

1 SPRINKLE the pork roast with flour that has been seasoned with salt and pepper.

2 PLACE vegetable oil in a skillet over high heat, until nearly smoking hot. Add floured pork, and brown, about 5 minutes. (You can also do this right in the crock of many modern slow cookers by using the cooker's browning function.)

3 REMOVE skillet from heat and deglaze the pan with the orange juice, scraping any browned bits from the bottom.

4 TRANSFER pork and all liquid from the skillet to a slow cooker and top with the teriyaki sauce, sesame oil, if desired, onion, carrots, garlic, thyme, and pepper.

5 SET the cooker to LOW, cover, and let cook 7 hours.

6 WHISK cornstarch into 2 tablespoons of water and stir into the cooking liquid. Add snow peas, re-cover, set the cooker to HIGH, and let cook 1 additional hour, or until meat is fork-tender.

7 TURN off heat and transfer roast to a cutting board to carve. Stir butter into the gravy, and serve roast smothered with the vegetables and gravy.

Italian Sausage Bolognese

Robust Flavors Brought Out of Simple Ingredients

This made-from-scratch red meat sauce is loaded with crumbled Italian sausage to introduce the wonderful flavors of pork and fennel to a Sunday standard.

Shopping List

2 tablespoons olive oil

1 pound ground Italian sausage

1 yellow onion, chopped

2 (14½-ounce) cans diced tomatoes, undrained

1 (15-ounce) can tomato sauce

1 (6-ounce) can tomato paste

3 tablespoons sugar

1 tablespoon minced garlic

1 tablespoon Italian seasoning

2 teaspoons balsamic vinegar

¾ teaspoon salt

¼ teaspoon pepper

1 PLACE olive oil in a large skillet over medium-high heat. Add Italian sausage, and cook until brown, about 5 minutes. (You can also do this right in the crock of many modern slow cookers by using the cooker's browning function.)

2 WHEN meat is almost browned, drain off any excess fat, return to heat, and add onion, cooking just until they sweat.

3 TRANSFER browned meat and onion to a slow cooker and cover with remaining ingredients, stirring to combine.

4 SET the cooker to LOW, cover, and let cook 8 hours before serving over your favorite pasta.

Helpful Tip

Doubling this recipe and serving over 2 pounds of pasta can feed a crowd of 10–12 in a pinch.

Kielbasa with Apples and Cabbage

A Family Meal, Ready When You Are

Smoky kielbasa sausage is perfectly matched with homemade sweet and sour cabbage in this family-pleasing dish. The addition of apples adds even more crunch and sweetness. Serve alongside potatoes for a full meal.

Shopping List

1 large yellow onion, thinly sliced

16 ounces kielbasa sausage, cut into 1-inch lengths

1 small head red cabbage, shredded

2 large apples, cored and cut into wedges

3 tablespoons butter or margarine

¼ cup cider vinegar

½ cup ketchup

1 tablespoon light brown sugar

¼ teaspoon garlic powder

¼ teaspoon salt

¼ teaspoon pepper

1 PLACE onion in a lightly greased skillet over medium-high heat, and sauté until lightly caramelized, about 5 minutes. (You can also do this right in the crock of many modern slow cookers by using the cooker's browning function.)

2 PLACE caramelized onion in a slow cooker and cover with remaining ingredients, stirring to combine.

3 SET the cooker to LOW, cover, and let cook 4 hours, or until ready to serve. Serve using a slotted spoon.

Make It Easier

You can also make this with a 16-ounce bag of shredded coleslaw cabbage in place of shredding your own red cabbage.

Pork Cassoulet

Topped with Crispy Bread Crumbs

Cassoulet is a southern French dish of meat and white beans. While typically made with duck, the Americanized version that this is based on uses three types of pork.

Shopping List

1 pound dried Great Nothern beans

4 slices bacon, chopped

1½ pounds boneless country-style ribs

8 ounces smoked sausage, sliced

1 yellow onion, chopped

3 cups chicken stock or broth

1 (14½-ounce) can diced tomatoes, drained

3 tablespoons tomato paste

1 tablespoon minced garlic

2 bay leaves

¾ teaspoon salt

½ teaspoon pepper

1 tablespoon butter or margarine

1 cup panko bread crumbs

Helpful Hint

Any boneless cuts of pork can be used in place of the country-style ribs, as long as you cut it into easy-to-serve pieces before cooking.

1 SOAK Great Northern beans overnight by placing in a large bowl and covering with cold water. Leave at least 3 inches of water for the beans to expand.

2 DRAIN and rinse the soaked beans and place in a slow cooker.

3 PLACE bacon in a skillet over high heat, and cook until bacon is crisp. Remove cooked bacon with a slotted spoon and reserve.

4 ADD country-style ribs to the bacon grease in the skillet, and brown on both sides, about 5 minutes. (You can also do this right in the crock of many modern slow cookers by using the cooker's browning function.)

5 TRANSFER browned ribs and reserved cooked bacon to the slow cooker, and cover with remaining ingredients, except butter and bread crumbs. Stir to combine.

6 SET the cooker to LOW, cover, and let cook 8 hours, or until beans and ribs are tender.

7 MELT butter in a skillet over medium-high heat and add bread crumbs, shaking the pan to toast them until they are golden brown.

8 SERVE Pork Cassoulet topped with the toasted bread crumbs.

Pork Chops with Onion Gravy

A Great Meal When Served over Buttered Noodles

Slow cookers work their magic best with proteins such as pork, which has a tendency to dry out during a typical cooking process. These chops cook as tender as can be in aromatic gravy, and the only disappointment is the moment that they disappear from the plate.

Shopping List

1 tablespoon vegetable oil

4 thick-cut pork chops, about 1¼ inches thick

Salt and pepper to taste

2 yellow onions, sliced thick

1½ cups beef stock or broth

2 tablespoons balsamic vinegar

1 tablespoon light brown sugar

1 teaspoon dry thyme

¼ teaspoon garlic powder

2 bay leaves

1 tablespoon cornstarch

3 tablespoons butter or margarine

Make It Better

Stir in ¼ cup of heavy cream, sour cream, or Greek yogurt in the last step for a creamier, richer gravy!

1 PLACE vegetable oil in a skillet over high heat, until nearly smoking hot. Generously season the pork chops with salt and pepper, place in the skillet, and brown on each side, about 5 minutes. (You can also do this right in the crock of many modern slow cookers by using the cooker's browning function.)

2 ADD the onions to the skillet, and then deglaze the pan with the beef stock, scraping any browned bits from the bottom.

3 TRANSFER pork, onions, and all liquid from the skillet to a slow cooker; top with the vinegar, sugar, thyme, garlic powder, and bay leaves.

4 SET the cooker to LOW, cover, and let cook 7 hours.

5 WHISK cornstarch into 2 tablespoons of water and stir into the cooking liquid. Re-cover, set the cooker to HIGH, and let cook 1 additional hour, or until meat is fork-tender.

6 TURN off heat, stir in the butter, and season gravy with salt and pepper to taste. Serve chops smothered with the onion gravy.

Prep Time	Cook Time	Temperature	Serves
15 min	7 hrs	Low	6-8

Ham with Apple Mustard Sauce

Because Ham, Fruit, and Mustard Were Meant to Be

This ham cooks in a light and sweet "gravy" made from apple juice and coarse deli mustard. Over the slow-cooking process, the flavors of apple and mustard infuse into the ham as the juices of the ham infuse into the sauce.

Shopping List

1 (3-pound) boneless ham

1 red apple, peeled and diced

¼ cup finely diced yellow onion

1 cup apple juice

¼ cup light brown sugar

3 tablespoons coarse deli mustard

2 tablespoons cornstarch

⅛ teaspoon ground cinnamon

1 PLACE ham at the bottom of a slow cooker, and cover with diced apple and onion.

2 WHISK together all remaining ingredients and pour over top of ham in slow cooker.

3 SET the cooker to LOW, cover, and let cook 7 hours, or until sauce is thickened and ham is warmed throughout.

4 SERVE ham sliced and topped with the Apple Mustard Sauce.

Make It Better

This is even better when made with apple cider in place of the apple juice, though cider isn't always sold year-round.

Dijon Beer Brats

Smothered in Onions and Red Cabbage

Bratwurst and beer have always been the best of buds. That's no exception when it comes to this easy-to-prepare German-style favorite, which gives everyone something more to root for come the Big Game.

Shopping List

2 pounds bratwurst, about 8 links

12 ounces beer (may use 2 teaspoons cider vinegar and 12 ounces water)

2 cups water

3 tablespoons whole-grain mustard

3 tablespoons light brown sugar

2 white onions, thinly sliced

½ head red cabbage, thinly sliced

1 PLACE bratwurst in a slow cooker and cover with remaining ingredients, tossing to combine.

2 SET the cooker to LOW, cover, and let cook 6 hours.

3 REMOVE bratwurst, leave whole or cut into thick slices, and serve on a platter tossed together with the cooked onions and cabbage, or as a filling in hearty buns.

Make It Better

Browning the bratwurst and onions in an oiled skillet over high heat (or using the browning function of many modern slow cookers) before slow cooking will add an additional level of flavor to this dish.

Mojo Pulled Pork

Tender Pork in a Cuban Citrus Marinade

Mojo is a marinade very much like Italian dressing, only infused with the tangy flavors of the Caribbean (as common in Miami as the shining sun), the result of which offers a roast so tender that it falls apart under the prongs of a fork.

Shopping List

1 (3- to 4-pound) pork roast

1 (16-ounce) bottle mojo criollo marinade (found in the Latin foods aisle)

Juice from 2 limes

1 teaspoon minced garlic

2 tablespoons chopped cilantro

2 tablespoons vegetable oil

1 cup chicken stock or broth

Helpful Tip

Though better when marinated and browned, you can skip these steps in a pinch, and just throw everything into the cooker from the start.

1 PLACE the roast in a large container with the mojo criollo, lime juice, garlic, and cilantro. Cover and let marinate in the refrigerator for at least 2 hours.

2 PLACE vegetable oil in a skillet over high heat, until nearly smoking hot. Remove roast from fridge and reserve the marinade. Place roast in skillet, and brown on both sides, about 5 minutes. (You can also do this right in the crock of many modern slow cookers by using the cooker's browning function.)

3 REMOVE the skillet from heat, and deglaze the pan with the chicken stock, scraping any browned bits from the bottom.

4 TRANSFER pork and all liquid from the skillet to a slow cooker and top with the reserved marinade.

5 SET the cooker to LOW, cover, and let cook 8–10 hours or until meat is fork-tender.

6 TURN off heat, remove roast, and shred into large chunks by fork. Serve dipped in the cooking liquid to keep moist.

Pork Carnitas

In Flour Tortillas with Tomato and Onion

This recipe for soft tacos filled with Pork Carnitas is far from authentic, but the flavors are all there. While this Mexican shredded pork is typically cooked twice, I've simplified things, though you can read my tip below to prepare it more traditionally.

Shopping List

1 (3- to 4-pound) pork roast

⅔ cup chicken stock or broth

1 cup chunky salsa

1 (4-ounce) can chopped green chiles, undrained

½ cup chopped cilantro

1 tablespoon minced garlic

1 teaspoon onion powder

½ teaspoon cumin

¾ teaspoon salt

½ teaspoon pepper

Flour tortillas, diced tomato, and diced red onion, to serve

1 SLICE pork roast in half and place in slow cooker.

2 COVER with all remaining ingredients, tossing to thoroughly coat each half.

3 SET the cooker to LOW, cover, and let cook 8 hours, or until meat is fork-tender.

4 USING 2 forks, shred the meat into the cooking sauce.

5 SERVE in warmed flour tortillas topped with diced tomato and diced red onion.

Make It Better

The pork in this is typically browned after cooking to bring out even more flavor. This can be done by shredding the meat onto a sheet pan (without sauce) and baking for 15 minutes at 400° before returning the meat to the sauce to serve.

Cranberry Pork Loin

Classic Holiday Slow Cooking

This easy holiday pork roast recipe cooks up in a cranberry sauce with fresh orange zest. Sage and a pinch of allspice add an earthiness that helps balance out the sweetness of the cranberry sauce.

Shopping List

1 (2- to 3-pound) pork loin roast

Salt and pepper to taste

2 (14-ounce) cans whole berry cranberry sauce

1 teaspoon orange zest

3 leaves sage, chopped

½ teaspoon onion powder

⅛ teaspoon allspice

1 GENEROUSLY season pork loin with salt and pepper, and place in a slow cooker.

2 ADD all remaining ingredients to the roast in the cooker.

3 SET the cooker to LOW, cover, and let cook 6 hours, or until a meat thermometer registers 160°.

4 REMOVE roast from slow cooker and let rest 5 minutes before slicing. Season the sauce with a pinch of salt and serve over the sliced pork.

Helpful Hint

Cooking 6 hours will leave the meat tender but still somewhat firm (similar to if it was oven-roasted). If you'd like pork that is literally fork-tender and falling apart as you slice it, cook at least 8 hours.

Sweet and Sour Ribs

Tender Ribs in an Irresistible Sauce

With a sauce reminiscent to barbecue and Asian sweet-and-sour, these delectable ribs will literally fall off the bone, melt in your mouth, and disappear before your very eyes.

Shopping List

3 pounds pork spareribs

Salt and pepper to taste

1 yellow onion, diced

1 (12-ounce) bottle ketchup

1 tablespoon cider vinegar

1 (15-ounce) can pineapple chunks, drained

2 tablespoons dark brown sugar

2 teaspoons minced garlic

1 tablespoon soy sauce

¼ teaspoon pepper

1   PREHEAT broiler and generously season ribs with salt and pepper.

2   PLACE ribs on a broiler pan, and broil on top rack of oven for 12–15 minutes, just until browned. Let cool 10 minutes.

3   MEANWHILE, add all remaining ingredients to a slow cooker and stir to combine.

4   CUT ribs into sections small enough to fit into your slow cooker, and add to the sauce in the cooker, tossing all to coat.

5   SET the cooker to LOW, cover, and let cook 5 hours, or until meat is fork-tender.

6   SERVE ribs topped with sauce and pineapples from the cooker.

Helpful Tip

If the sauce is too watery before serving, simply ladle it into a saucepot over high heat and add 1 teaspoon of cornstarch whisked into 2 tablespoons of water. Let simmer 2 minutes to thicken.

Pork Tenderloin with Mushroom Gravy

The Leanest Cut of Pork in a Creamy, Reduced-Fat Gravy

As the leanest, most tender cut of pork, tenderloin is fondly known as the "filet mignon" of the other white meat. This recipe highlights the tenderloin by smothering it in creamy mushroom gravy.

Shopping List

2 pork tenderloins (about 1 pound each)

Salt and pepper to taste

2 tablespoons olive oil

1 cup chicken stock or broth

¼ cup white wine (may use 2 tablespoons white wine vinegar)

½ red onion, diced

8 ounces sliced button mushrooms

2 teaspoons minced garlic

2 teaspoons dry tarragon

1 teaspoon Dijon mustard

1½ cups reduced-fat sour cream

Make It a Meal

Believe it or not, grits make a great side dish to serve right under the pork and gravy.

1 SEASON the pork tenderloins generously with salt and pepper.

2 PLACE olive oil in a skillet over high heat, until almost smoking hot. Add tenderloins, and brown on all sides, about 5 minutes. (You can also do this right in the crock of many modern slow cookers by using the cooker's browning function.)

3 REMOVE skillet from heat and deglaze the pan with the chicken stock, scraping any browned bits from the bottom.

4 TRANSFER tenderloins and all liquid from the skillet to a slow cooker. Top with white wine, onion, mushrooms, garlic, and tarragon.

5 SET the cooker to LOW, cover, and let cook 8 hours.

6 TURN off heat, transfer tenderloins to a cutting board, and stir mustard and sour cream into the gravy. Add salt and pepper to taste.

7 CARVE pork into thick slices and serve topped with mushroom gravy.

Bacon and Apple Stuffed Pork

Holiday Flavors, All Wrapped Up

This pork loin roast is pounded thin, filled with apple, bacon, onion, and sage, and then rolled up into a beautiful pinwheel before cooking. The apple and sage are not just a great complement to the pork, but very traditional holiday flavors, making this a wonderful dish to serve come the end of the year.

Shopping List

1 (2-pound) pork loin roast

Salt and pepper to taste

1 apple, peeled and finely diced

⅓ cup finely diced yellow onion

½ cup cooked bacon pieces

4 leaves sage, chopped

1 teaspoon minced garlic

1 cup apple juice

3 tablespoons butter or margarine

½ teaspoon dried thyme

Make It Easier

Tie the rolled pork in 3 places with baking twine to make transferring into the cooker easier, and ensure the pork will hold its shape as it cooks.

1 BUTTERFLY pork loin by slicing down its entire length about ¾ of the way through. Lay the butterflied pork loin between 2 sheets of plastic wrap and pound with a meat mallet until flattened to about ⅓ inch thick.

2 GENEROUSLY season both sides of the pounded pork with salt and pepper.

3 COMBINE apple, onion, bacon, sage, and garlic to create a filling.

4 SPOON the filling over the entire surface of the pork loin, and then roll up into a pinwheel.

5 PLACE stuffed pork into a slow cooker, seam side down.

6 ADD apple juice, butter, and thyme to the cooker.

7 SET the cooker to LOW, cover, and let cook 8 hours.

8 REMOVE from slow cooker and let rest 10 minutes before slicing. Season the cooking liquid with salt and pepper, and serve drizzled over the sliced pork.

Vegetables and Sides

Slow-Roasted Potatoes

The Perfect Little Potatoes That Set Your Oven Free

I love roasted potatoes, especially baby potatoes like those used in this recipe, but I typically roast them in the oven at 450°. That creates major problems when I need my oven at a lower temperature to cook the rest of the meal. This recipe takes those potatoes out of the oven and into the slow cooker with a crispy-skin result you'd never think was possible at such a low temperature.

Shopping List

3 pounds baby potatoes

1 tablespoon extra virgin olive oil

2 teaspoons chopped fresh
  rosemary leaves

¼ teaspoon garlic powder

½ teaspoon salt

¼ teaspoon pepper

3 tablespoons grated Parmesan
  cheese

1 ADD all ingredients, except Parmesan cheese, to a slow cooker and toss to combine.

2 SET the cooker to HIGH, cover, and let cook 2 hours, stirring halfway through. Cook until potatoes are crispy on the outside and fork-tender.

3 TOSS with the Parmesan cheese just before serving.

Helpful Tip

Baby Yukon gold potatoes are creamy, delicious, and perfect for this recipe. Many stores also carry mixed baby potatoes that are gold, red, and purple in the same bag—the taste between the three is negligible, but the presentation is very nice.

Chili-Spiced Succotash

A Bright Side Dish That's Full of Flavor

Succotash is often a very boring, flavorless combination of vegetables best left to cafeterias—but this version is anything but that! With all the spices of chili, I've made succotash into a hearty side that will have you going back for seconds.

Shopping List

1 (16-ounce) bag frozen corn kernels

1 (16-ounce) bag frozen lima beans

1 (16-ounce) bag frozen green beans

1 red onion, diced

1 (28-ounce) can diced tomatoes, undrained

2 tablespoons butter or margarine

2 teaspoons paprika

2 teaspoons chili powder

½ teaspoon garlic powder

½ teaspoon onion powder

¼ teaspoon cayenne pepper

1 teaspoon salt

½ teaspoon pepper

1 PLACE all ingredients into a slow cooker and toss to combine.

2 SET the cooker to LOW, cover, and let cook 6 hours, or until lima beans are as tender as you like them.

Make It a Meal

Adding 1 pound of browned ground beef, ¼ cup beef stock, and 6–8 quartered red bliss potatoes in the first step will turn this side dish into an entire family meal.

Southwestern Creamed Corn

A Somewhat-Spicy Twist on a Classic

Nothing can add a homey mood to a meal quite like a heaping portion of creamed corn, especially if it kicks the mouth with southwestern flavor. If you really like things spicy, feel free to leave the seeds of the jalapeño in the mix to add heat.

Shopping List

32 ounces frozen corn kernels

1 cup evaporated milk

2 teaspoons cornstarch

1 (8-ounce) brick cream cheese, cubed

2 tablespoons butter or margarine

½ cup diced red bell pepper

1 jalapeño pepper, seeded and finely diced

1 tablespoon sugar

2 teaspoons chili powder

½ teaspoon salt

1 PLACE corn kernels in a slow cooker.

2 WHISK together evaporated milk and cornstarch, and pour over corn kernels in the cooker.

3 COVER with remaining ingredients and stir to combine.

4 SET the cooker to LOW, cover, and let cook 3–4 hours, or until corn is hot throughout, and sauce is bubbling hot. Stir well before serving.

Make It Different

You can make this into a standard version of creamed corn by simply omitting the red bell pepper, jalapeño, and chili powder.

Candied Beets

I Say It's Time to Revisit This Root Veggie

Though you may want to put on some gloves before cutting into fresh beets to keep your hands from turning, well, beet-red, the effort will be very much rewarded. Beets are often overlooked, but can be a delicious and eye-appealing side dish when well prepared.

Shopping List

4–6 small to medium beets

2 tablespoons butter or margarine

3 tablespoons light brown sugar

¼ cup water

1 teaspoon orange zest

¼ teaspoon salt

1 PEEL and slice beets into thin slices, about ¼ inch thick.

2 PLACE sliced beets in a slow cooker and cover with remaining ingredients, stirring to combine.

3 SET the cooker to LOW, cover, and let cook 5–6 hours, or until beets are fork-tender.

4 SERVE garnished with additional orange zest, if desired.

Make It Better

Try adding a sprig of fresh tarragon to the slow cooker before cooking to infuse a subtle, almost licorice flavor into the sweet beets. Or try adding a handful of real bacon bits before cooking for a smoky and savory contrast to the beets.

Ratatouille Parmesan

A Twist on the Slow-Roasted French Side Dish

This recipe melds French ratatouille with Italian lasagna to create a delicious dish layered with vegetables, red sauce, and ricotta cheese.

Shopping List

1 large eggplant, cubed

2 yellow onions, sliced thick

3 large zucchini, sliced

3 large tomatoes, sliced thick

1 red bell pepper, diced

Italian seasoning

Salt and pepper to taste

1 cup pizza sauce

1 (6-ounce) can tomato paste

16 ounces ricotta cheese

1 large egg

½ cup grated Parmesan cheese

1 Spray a slow cooker with nonstick cooking spray.

2 Layer ⅓ of the eggplant, onions, zucchini, tomatoes, and red bell pepper in the bottom of the slow cooker, and sprinkle with a generous amount of Italian seasoning, salt, and pepper.

3 Whisk together pizza sauce and tomato paste and spoon ⅓ of the mixture over top the seasoned vegetables.

4 Whisk together ricotta cheese, egg, and Parmesan cheese, and spoon ⅓ of the mixture over the sauced vegetables.

5 Repeat for 2 more layers of seasoned vegetables, then sauce, then cheese, ending with the cheese on top.

6 Set the cooker to LOW, cover, and let cook 8 hours.

Helpful Hint

Pasta sauce can be used in place of the pizza sauce, but I find that pizza sauce is thicker and holds up better to the water released by the vegetables as they cook.

Slow Cooker Stuffing

Saving Precious Holiday Stove Top/Oven Real Estate

Gear up for the holidays painlessly by preparing turkey's best sidekick away from everything else in the oven. By the time you smell the thyme, the table will be set, and you'll have forgotten that the perfect stuffing had been taking care of itself.

Shopping List

12 cups cubed, toasted bread

1 tablespoon vegetable oil

1 large yellow onion, diced

1 cup diced celery

¼ cup butter (½ stick), melted

1¾ cups chicken stock or broth

2 large eggs

1 tablespoon poultry seasoning

½ teaspoon dried thyme

1 teaspoon onion powder

1 teaspoon salt

½ teaspoon pepper

Helpful Hint

Toasted sandwich bread can be used in this recipe, but French or Italian (crusty) bread will be even better. Chop into cubes and bake at 300° for 5–10 minutes, just until lightly browned before preparing the stuffing.

1 IF using a 4-quart slow cooker, place cubed bread in a large mixing bowl or stockpot. If using a larger slow cooker, you can place the bread directly into the cooker.

2 PLACE vegetable oil, onion, and celery in a skillet over medium-high heat, and sauté until vegetables sweat, about 4 minutes. (You can also do this right in the crock of many modern slow cookers by using the cooker's browning function.)

3 TRANSFER cooked vegetables to the cubed bread. Whisk together remaining ingredients and pour over top of all, tossing to combine and moisten bread.

4 PACK the moistened stuffing mixture into a slow cooker, cover, and set the cooker to HIGH.

5 LET cook 1 hour before lowering the cooker to LOW and cooking an additional 4 hours, or until stuffing is crispy on the edges and hot throughout.

Barley and Mushroom Pilaf

The Perfect Mix of Whole-Grain Barley and Brown Rice

Rice pilaf can be either a simple or complex pairing for just about any protein. Reminiscent of the flavors of cream of mushroom soup, this particular version rings with the earthy tone of barley and baby bella mushrooms.

Shopping List

1 tablespoon olive oil

1 small yellow onion, diced

1 carrot, peeled and diced

8 ounces baby bella mushrooms, chopped

⅔ cup brown rice

5½ cups beef stock or broth

1 cup pearl barley

1 sprig fresh rosemary

1 tablespoon minced garlic

½ teaspoon onion powder

¼ teaspoon pepper

2 tablespoons butter or margarine

2 tablespoons chopped parsley

Salt to taste

1 PLACE olive oil, onion, carrot, and mushrooms in a large skillet over medium-high heat, and sauté until onion and mushrooms are lightly browned, about 5 minutes. (You can also do this right in the crock of many modern slow cookers by using the cooker's browning function.)

2 ADD brown rice to the skillet and sauté just 1 minute longer.

3 DEGLAZE the skillet with some of the beef broth, and then transfer all to a slow cooker. Add remaining beef broth, barley, whole rosemary sprig, garlic, onion powder, and pepper.

4 SET the cooker to LOW, cover, and let cook 5–6 hours, or until rice and barley are tender.

5 STIR in butter or margarine, parsley, and salt to taste before serving.

Helpful Hint

You can also make this with only barley by adding 1⅓ cups pearl barley and omitting the brown rice.

Cheesy Polenta

Italian Grits with Cheddar Cheese

Polenta is just now starting to truly catch on in restaurants in America. Usually served underneath a savory meat like roasted and sliced pork, my recipe is simple and absolutely delicious. Look for coarse cornmeal or dry polenta that isn't labeled "instant" or "quick cooking" for the proper results.

Shopping List

2 cups coarse cornmeal

3 cups chicken stock or broth

3½ cups water

3 tablespoons butter or margarine

1 teaspoon salt

¼ teaspoon garlic powder

8 ounces shredded sharp Cheddar cheese

1 PLACE cornmeal, chicken broth, water, butter, salt, and garlic powder in a slow cooker and stir to combine.

2 SET the cooker to HIGH, cover, and let cook 1 hour.

3 STIR in Cheddar cheese, re-cover, and cook 1 additional hour before serving.

Helpful Tip

This should be a creamy, oatmeal-like consistency, but it can over-thicken quickly as it sits. If this happens, simply thin it back out with milk or water.

Bacon and Brown Sugar Green Beans

A Classic Combination of Flavors

This snappy side dish, cooked just until the beans are as tender as you like them, mingles sweet brown sugar and savory bacon.

Shopping List

4 slices thick-cut bacon, chopped

1 small yellow onion, diced

1 pound fresh green beans, ends snapped

¼ cup water

2 tablespoons light brown sugar

1 tablespoon butter or margarine

2 teaspoons minced garlic

1 teaspoon red wine vinegar

½ teaspoon onion powder

½ teaspoon salt

1 PLACE bacon and onion in a skillet over medium-high heat, and sauté until bacon is crispy and onion is caramelized, about 7 minutes. (You can also do this right in the crock of many modern slow cookers by using the cooker's browning function.) Drain and discard ⅔ of the bacon grease.

2 TRANSFER bacon and onions and the remaining ⅓ of bacon grease to a slow cooker, and cover with remaining ingredients.

3 SET the cooker to LOW, cover, and let cook 3 hours, or until green beans are as tender as you like them.

Helpful Hint

Cider or balsamic vinegar can be used in place of the red wine vinegar, if you don't have any red wine vinegar on hand.

Barbecue Lima Beans

With Barbecue Sauce Made Entirely from Scratch

Most people are not that fond of lima beans, but I'm guessing they haven't tried them in a recipe like this one! I actually find that they make barbecue baked beans heartier and more "toothsome" than the usual small white beans that have a tendency to get mushy.

Shopping List

16 ounces dried baby lima beans

5 strips thick-cut bacon, chopped (optional)

1 yellow onion, diced

3 cups water

1 cup ketchup

½ cup dark brown sugar

⅓ cup red wine vinegar

3 tablespoons Dijon mustard

1 tablespoon Worcestershire sauce

2 teaspoons paprika

½ teaspoon garlic powder

1 teaspoon salt

1 teaspoon pepper

1 Soak baby lima beans overnight by placing in a large bowl and covering with cold water. Leave at least 3 inches of water for the beans to expand.

2 Drain and rinse the soaked beans and place in a slow cooker.

3 Cover beans with remaining ingredients and stir to combine.

4 Set the cooker to LOW, cover, and let cook 8 hours, or until beans are tender.

Make It Better

This is even better if you substitute 2 cups of root beer for 2 of the cups of water. Cut the brown sugar down to ⅓ of a cup to account for the extra sugar in the soda.

Southern Corn Pudding

Like Cornbread, Only Better

Corn pudding is a creamy, sweet and savory spoon bread made in the style of cornbread. My recipe includes tons of whole-kernel corn for crunch, and creamed corn and cream cheese for creaminess.

Shopping List

1 (8-ounce) brick cream cheese

1 (8½-ounce) package corn muffin mix

1 cup milk

2 large eggs, beaten

¼ cup sugar

2 tablespoons vegetable oil

2 cups frozen corn kernels

1 (16-ounce) can creamed corn

¾ teaspoon salt

1 MICROWAVE cream cheese for 30 seconds, just until it begins to melt.

2 COMBINE melted cream cheese, corn muffin mix, milk, eggs, sugar, and oil, and use an electric beater to beat until smooth.

3 FOLD in remaining ingredients.

4 SPRAY a slow cooker with nonstick cooking spray before pouring the corn batter into the cooker.

5 SET the cooker to HIGH, cover, and let cook 2 hours.

6 SWITCH cooker to LOW and cook an additional 3 hours before spooning out of the cooker to serve.

Helpful Tip

The edges of this will brown, but don't be alarmed—that's the really good stuff!

Green Bean Casserole

With Fresh Baby Bella Mushrooms

Just about everyone has had this traditional side dish at one time or another. Usually, it's during the holidays, but really, when else can condensed cream soup make something so tasty? When the cans stare at you in the aisle of the grocery store, don't fight it. Feel free to make this casserole all year-round!

Shopping List

2 teaspoons vegetable oil

1 yellow onion, diced

8 ounces baby bella mushrooms, chopped

2 tablespoons butter or margarine

1 teaspoon beef base, or 1 beef bouillon cube

1 pound fresh green beans, ends snapped

1 (10¾-ounce) can cream of celery soup

½ cup evaporated milk

½ cup grated Parmesan cheese

½ teaspoon onion powder

¼ teaspoon garlic powder

¼ teaspoon pepper

Salt to taste

1¼ cups French-fried onions

1 PLACE vegetable oil, onion, and mushrooms in a skillet over medium-high heat, and sauté until onions begin to caramelize, about 5 minutes. (You can also do this right in the crock of many modern slow cookers by using the cooker's browning function.) Remove from heat and add butter and beef base, just to melt.

2 PLACE the cooked vegetable mixture, green beans, cream of celery soup, evaporated milk, Parmesan cheese, onion powder, garlic powder, and pepper into the crock of a slow cooker and stir to combine.

3 SET the cooker to LOW, cover, and let cook 4 hours.

4 UNCOVER and season with salt to taste. Sprinkle French-fried onions over top and continue cooking uncovered 1 hour, or until green beans are as tender as you like them.

Make It Yours

Any condensed cream soup can be used in this recipe, though I find that cream of celery comes out tasting the most homemade when combined with the fresh mushrooms and other ingredients.

Scalloped Potatoes

No Oven Necessary

Scalloped Potatoes are one of my favorite sides to prepare in the slow cooker for one simple reason—the potatoes always come out tender! I can't tell you how many times I've over-browned them in the oven, only to find that the potatoes were still crunchy and undercooked. Thankfully, with this recipe, that's a thing of the past.

Shopping List

6 russet potatoes

3 tablespoons butter or margarine, melted

½ cup sliced green onions

1 cup shredded Cheddar-Jack cheese

1½ cups whole milk

3 tablespoons all-purpose flour

⅛ teaspoon nutmeg

¾ teaspoon salt

½ teaspoon pepper

1 PEEL and cut potatoes into ⅙-inch slices. Toss all potato slices in the melted butter.

2 SPRAY a slow cooker with nonstick cooking spray and then place ⅓ of the coated potatoes on the bottom. Top with ⅓ of the green onions and ⅓ of the Cheddar-Jack cheese. Repeat to make 3 layers, pouring any remaining butter over top.

3 WHISK together remaining ingredients and pour over the layered potatoes and cheese in slow cooker.

4 SET the cooker to LOW, cover, and let cook 8 hours, or until potatoes are tender.

Make It Yours

Any shredded cheese works well in this recipe in place of the Cheddar-Jack, especially Swiss cheese. If you can't find it shredded, simply place a layer of sliced Swiss cheese in between each layer of potatoes.

Glazed Carrots

With Orange Zest and a Touch of Vanilla

These taproots are simmered to soft perfection, coated in a sweet glaze, and will leave you clearly seeing that side dishes don't have to be a boring bed of vegetables. The possibilities for pairing are endless!

Shopping List

32 ounces baby carrots

1 cup orange juice

¼ cup dark brown sugar

2 tablespoons butter or margarine

1 teaspoon orange zest

½ teaspoon ground cinnamon

¼ teaspoon vanilla extract

¼ teaspoon salt

1 tablespoon cornstarch

1 PLACE all ingredients, except cornstarch, into a slow cooker and toss well.

2 SET the cooker to LOW, cover, and let cook 4 hours.

3 WHISK cornstarch into 2 tablespoons of water and stir into cooker.

4 SET the cooker to HIGH, cover, and let cook 1 additional hour before serving.

Make It Different

You can also make "Apple Pie Glazed Carrots" by using apple juice in place of the orange juice, and ¾ teaspoon of apple pie spice in place of the orange zest and ground cinnamon.

Fried Apples

A Great Southern Side . . . or Is It Dessert?

Magic things happen when apples are cooked slow, especially in this classic southern side dish that is more of a dessert than your typical side. Just don't forget the lemons! Lemon juice helps keep them from oxidizing and turning brown during the cooking process.

Shopping List

4 large green apples, peeled, cored, and cut into wedges

1 tablespoon lemon juice

2 tablespoons cornstarch

⅓ cup light brown sugar

¼ cup sugar

½ teaspoon ground cinnamon

¼ teaspoon allspice

¼ teaspoon salt

¼ cup melted butter

1 Toss apples in lemon juice as you cut them.

2 Spray the insert of your slow cooker with nonstick cooking spray.

3 Cover apples with cornstarch and toss to evenly coat. Transfer to the greased slow cooker.

4 Add remaining ingredients and stir to combine.

5 Set the cooker to HIGH, cover, and let cook about 3 hours, stirring occasionally, until apples are tender.

Make It Memorable

Believe it or not, adding a few slices of chopped, cooked bacon to these fried apples makes them even more delicious, even when serving as a dessert!

Risotto Primavera

Creamy Rice with Vibrant Vegetables

Anybody who has read any of my pressure cooking cookbooks knows that I absolutely love making risotto, especially when I don't have to be constantly stirring it on the stove! This Risotto Primavera is made with broccoli, peas, and red bell pepper for a dish that's as beautiful as it is delicious.

Shopping List

1¼ cups short-grain (Arborio) rice

3 tablespoons olive oil

2 cups frozen broccoli florets

⅔ cup frozen peas

4 cups chicken stock or broth

1 yellow onion, diced

¼ cup finely diced red bell pepper

1 teaspoon minced garlic

¾ teaspoon salt

¼ teaspoon pepper

⅔ cup grated Parmesan cheese

1 TOSS rice in olive oil to coat.

2 PLACE all ingredients, except Parmesan cheese, in the crock of a slow cooker.

3 SET cooker to LOW, cover, and let cook 2½ hours, or until rice is tender.

4 STIR in Parmesan cheese and let rest uncovered for 10 minutes to thicken before serving.

Make It Better

For a more authentic risotto, replace ½ cup of the chicken stock with dry white wine.

Desserts

Strawberry Jam

Because Nothing Tastes Better Than Homemade

Making homemade jams is a lot easier than people think, and using a slow cooker ensures that your spreadable edibles won't burn as they cook. While this recipe also includes jar-sealing instructions, you can skip this step if you plan on giving jars away to friends. Unsealed jam jars should be refrigerated and used within a few weeks.

Shopping List

4 pounds strawberries

1 (1¾-ounce) box powdered fruit pectin

6 cups sugar

3 tablespoons lemon juice

Make It Perfect

Due to variations in berry ripeness, you should test to see if the jam will set before jarring. Place a small amount of the cooked jam in a small dish and let cool in the freezer to check consistency. If not setting well, transfer jam to the stove, add ½ cup sugar, and bring to a rapid boil for 10 minutes.

1 HULL strawberries and quarter or roughly chop them, adding them to a slow cooker as you go.

2 USE a potato masher or heavy spoon to mash strawberries until they are sitting in their own juice, but still chunky.

3 COVER strawberries with remaining ingredients and stir to combine.

4 SET the cooker to HIGH, cover, and let cook 4 hours. Do not uncover while cooking.

5 BE sure the jam is simmering before turning off the heat. Immediately spoon into hot, sterile canning jars, leaving ¼ inch of headspace, and seal or keep refrigerated.

6 To seal, submerge jars in water and bring to a rapid boil for 5 minutes.

Bananas Foster

All the Flavor, Without Having to Set It on Fire!

With a scoop of vanilla ice cream melting on top of this bubbling-hot dessert, no one can deny the banana as the king of fruits. Unlike the usual restaurant preparation, flambéing (thankfully) isn't required.

Shopping List

4 large bananas, peeled

3 tablespoons butter or margarine, melted

½ cup light brown sugar

2 tablespoons water

1 teaspoon vanilla extract

¾ teaspoon rum extract

½ teaspoon ground cinnamon

¼ cup chopped pecans (optional)

Vanilla ice cream, to top

1 SLICE the bananas on a bias (diagonal), about ⅓ inch thick to make slightly oval discs.

2 PLACE sliced bananas and all other ingredients, except ice cream, in the crock of a slow cooker and toss to combine.

3 SET the cooker to LOW, cover, and let cook 2 hours, or until bubbling hot.

4 SERVE hot, topped with vanilla ice cream.

Make It Memorable

This is even better when served over shortcake and then topped with the vanilla ice cream. It gives you something to sop up the sauce and melted ice cream.

Chocolate Fondue

Kept Warm to Keep the Party Going

While I'll admit that Chocolate Fondue is almost more about what you dip into it than the chocolate itself, this is a very good recipe to know for parties and get-togethers. As for what to dip into it, try marshmallows, pretzels, shortbread cookies, strawberries, orange segments, graham crackers, or even bite-sized brownies.

Shopping List

Slow cooker liner (recommended)

2 cups semisweet chocolate chips

2 cups milk chocolate chips

1 cup heavy cream

⅓ cup milk

½ teaspoon vanilla extract

1 SECURE a slow cooker liner in your cooker for easier cleanup. Spray liner with nonstick cooking spray.

2 ADD all ingredients to lined slow cooker and toss to combine.

3 SET the cooker to LOW, cover, and let cook 1 hour, stirring halfway through.

4 STIR well and set cooker to WARM before serving right out of the cooker. If the fondue thickens over time, simply add a few tablespoons of milk to thin it out.

Make It Yours

This standard fondue recipe can be spiced up by adding just about anything that goes with chocolate. Try 2 teaspoons of orange zest, a pinch of cinnamon, or even a tablespoon of instant coffee granules for 3 different variations.

Cherry Cheesecake Rice Pudding

It's Easier to Make Than You'd Think

This rice pudding is made with cream cheese and extra vanilla extract to bring out the flavors and creaminess of cheesecake. It's then topped with a spoonful of cherry pie filling, just as many diners and restaurants classically serve their cheesecake.

Shopping List

6 cups 2% (reduced-fat) milk

¾ cup long-grain white rice

1 cup sugar

2 large eggs

¼ cup half-and-half

2 teaspoons vanilla extract

1 pinch salt

1 (8-ounce) brick cream cheese, sliced

1 (21-ounce) can cherry pie filling

Helpful Hint

If the pudding over-thickens, simply thin out with additional milk, just until it has reached your desired consistency.

1 PLACE milk, rice, and sugar in the crock of a slow cooker and stir to combine.

2 SET cooker to HIGH, cover, and let cook 30 minutes.

3 STIR, reduce cooker to LOW, cover, and let cook 5 additional hours

4 IN a mixing bowl, thoroughly whisk eggs, half-and-half, vanilla extract, and salt. Continue whisking as you spoon in a large spoonful of the hot rice mixture. Once combined, whisk another spoonful of the hot rice mixture into the egg mixture. This will keep the eggs from curdling in the next step.

5 THOROUGHLY fold the egg mixture into the remaining rice mixture in the slow cooker. Then stir in cream cheese.

6 SET cooker to HIGH, cover, and let cook 30 additional minutes, or until rice is tender and pudding has thickened. Stir every 15 minutes to prevent scorching as the pudding thickens.

7 SERVE warm or chilled, topped with a large dollop of the cherry pie filling.

Peanut Butter Cup Bread Pudding

Everyone's Favorite Candy in a Pudding

Chocolate and peanut butter are a universally loved combination that comes together in this bread pudding to create a flavor that reminds me of peanut butter cups. Top with chopped peanuts and chocolate syrup or hot fudge to really bring those flavors home.

Shopping List

6 cups cubed bread

⅔ cup semisweet chocolate chips

1 cup peanut butter morsels

6 large eggs

1 (12-ounce) can evaporated milk

½ cup half-and-half

¼ cup butter (½ stick), melted

1 cup light brown sugar

¼ cup sugar

2 teaspoons vanilla extract

1 pinch salt

Chopped peanuts and chocolate syrup, to serve

1 SPRAY a slow cooker with nonstick cooking spray.

2 LAYER ⅓ of the bread, then ⅓ of chocolate chips, then ⅓ of the peanut butter morsels at the bottom of the slow cooker. Repeat 2 more times to create 3 layers.

3 WHISK together eggs, evaporated milk, half-and-half, butter, brown sugar, sugar, vanilla extract, and salt. Pour over top of all in slow cooker.

4 SET the cooker to HIGH, cover, and let cook 1 hour.

5 SWITCH the cooker LOW and cook an additional 3 hours or until eggs have set throughout.

6 SERVE topped with chopped peanuts, and drizzled with chocolate syrup.

Helpful Hint

Sturdy (and especially stale) bread works best in bread pudding. Try French, challah, or even toasted 100% whole-wheat sandwich bread.

"Baked" Apples

Stuffed with Walnuts and Raisins

These warm, spiced apples are a delight any time of year, but especially perfect during the apple-picking months, when pies have taken up too much space on the kitchen window sill, and baking seems like too much work.

Shopping List

4 medium red apples

3 tablespoons butter or margarine, melted

½ cup raisins

¼ cup chopped walnuts

¼ cup dark brown sugar

½ teaspoon apple pie spice

1 CORE the apples, being careful not to go all the way through to the bottom of the apple. This should create a cavity in each for you to stuff with the remaining ingredients.

2 COMBINE the remaining ingredients, and spoon an equal amount into the openings of each apple.

3 SET the cooker to LOW, cover, and let cook 2 hours, or until apples are tender.

4 SERVE warm as is or beside a scoop of vanilla ice cream.

Make It Memorable

For a better presentation, use an apple peeler to peel the tops of each apple before filling with the other ingredients.

Prep Time	Cook Time	Temperature	Serves
20 min	2 hrs	High	6-8

Mixed Berry Cobbler

Cooked Upside Down in the Slow Cooker

A homemade cobbler beats any store-bought treat any day of the week! And since it's easier than pie, and even easier in the slow cooker, you can make this any day of the week.

Shopping List

BATTER

1 cup all-purpose flour

¾ cup sugar

1 teaspoon baking powder

¼ teaspoon ground cinnamon

1 pinch salt

2 large eggs

2 tablespoons butter, melted

2 tablespoons milk

1 tablespoon vegetable oil

Nonstick cooking spray

BERRIES

16 ounces frozen raspberries

16 ounces frozen blueberries

¾ cup sugar

1 tablespoon cornstarch, whisked into ¾ cup water

1 CREATE the BATTER by combining flour, sugar, baking powder, cinnamon, and salt in a large mixing bowl. In a separate mixing bowl, whisk together eggs, butter, milk, and vegetable oil. Fold the liquid mixture into the dry ingredients until all is combined.

2 SPRAY the crock of a slow cooker with non-stick cooking spray and then pour BATTER into the bottom.

3 PLACE all BERRIES ingredients in a sauce-pot over medium-high heat and bring to a boil.

4 POUR the boiling berry mixture over top of the BATTER in the slow cooker. Set the cooker to HIGH, cover, and let cook 2 hours.

5 REMOVE cover and let cool in cooker at least 15 minutes, to thicken, before serving.

Make It Yours

Any combination of 32 ounces (4 cups) of fresh or frozen berries will work in this cobbler, though I do not suggest using only strawberries on their own.

Real Tapioca Pudding

Truly Worth Making from Scratch

There is something quite rewarding when making tapioca pudding from scratch. With a simple vanilla flavor, this sweet treat has a texture all its own.

Shopping List

½ cup "small pearl" tapioca

4 cups 2% (reduced-fat) milk

¾ cup sugar

½ teaspoon vanilla extract

1 pinch salt

2 large eggs

Helpful Hint

Small pearl tapioca can usually be found in the health food or grains section of the grocery store. It may even be hiding in the gluten-free baking mixes section.

1 PLACE all ingredients, except eggs, in the crock of a slow cooker and stir to combine.

2 SET cooker to HIGH, cover, and let cook 2 hours.

3 IN a mixing bowl, thoroughly whisk eggs. Continue whisking as you spoon in a large spoonful of the hot tapioca mixture. Once combined, whisk another spoonful of the hot tapioca mixture into the eggs. This will keep the eggs from curdling in the next step.

4 THOROUGHLY fold the egg mixture into the remaining tapioca mixture in the slow cooker.

5 COVER and let cook 30 additional minutes, or until tapioca pearls are plump and translucent and pudding is thick. Stir every 15 minutes to prevent scorching as the pudding thickens.

6 SERVE warm or chilled.

Tropical Fruit Compote

With Mango, Pineapple, and Papaya

Friendly warning: Upon the first spoonful, this blend of pineapple, papaya, and mango pieces cooked in mango nectar, rum extract, and vanilla may make you feel as though an island breeze has just blown in from nowhere.

Shopping List

1 (16-ounce) bag frozen mango chunks

1 (16-ounce) bag frozen pineapple chunks

1 (16-ounce) bag frozen papaya chunks

1 cup mango nectar

3 tablespoons dark brown sugar

2 teaspoons cornstarch

¾ teaspoon vanilla extract

½ teaspoon rum extract

⅛ teaspoon ground cinnamon

⅛ teaspoon ground allspice

1 PLACE frozen fruit in the crock of a slow cooker.

2 WHISK together remaining ingredients and pour over fruit in the cooker, tossing to combine.

3 SET the cooker to HIGH, cover, and let cook 3 hours, or until bubbling hot.

4 SERVE warm, topped with vanilla ice cream or lemon sorbet. Or serve over angel food cake with a dollop of whipped cream.

Helpful Hint

While frozen mango and pineapple chunks are easy to find in the frozen fruit/smoothie ingredient section, if you cannot find papaya, a good substitution is frozen peach slices.

Banana Pecan Bread Pudding

Drizzled with Caramel Sauce

Bread puddings are not just a staple of slow cooking, but a staple of mine no matter how they're prepared. This bread pudding is loaded with fresh bananas and pecans, and topped with caramel sauce for a pudding that is like a marriage of both bananas Foster and butter pecan ice cream. In fact, it's even better when actually topped with butter pecan ice cream.

Shopping List

6 cups cubed bread

3 bananas, sliced

1 cup chopped pecans

6 large eggs

1 (12-ounce) can evaporated milk

½ cup half-and-half

¼ cup butter (½ stick), melted

1 cup light brown sugar

½ cup sugar

2 teaspoons vanilla extract

1 teaspoon ground cinnamon

1 pinch salt

Caramel sundae sauce, to serve

1 SPRAY a slow cooker with nonstick cooking spray.

2 PLACE bread, bananas, and pecans in the slow cooker and toss to combine.

3 WHISK together eggs, evaporated milk, half-and-half, butter, brown sugar, sugar, vanilla extract, cinnamon, and salt. Pour over top of all in slow cooker.

4 SET the cooker to HIGH, cover, and let cook 1 hour.

5 SWITCH the cooker to LOW and cook an additional 3 hours, or until eggs have set throughout.

6 SERVE drizzled with caramel sundae sauce.

Helpful Hint

Sturdy (and especially stale) bread works best in bread pudding. Try French, challah, or even toasted 100% whole-wheat sandwich bread.

Caramel Apple Crisp

Like a Caramel Apple That's Far Friendlier to Your Teeth

This Caramel Apple Crisp has all the flavors of a carnival caramel apple, but in a far easier-to-eat and more refined form. Chewy caramel candies are melted right between the apples and the crisp, for a dessert that is far more decadent than your average warm fruit desserts.

Shopping List

APPLES

5 large Granny Smith apples, peeled, cored, and chopped

1 tablespoon cornstarch

¼ cup sugar

1 tablespoon lemon juice

1 tablespoon water

¾ teaspoon apple pie spice

1 cup (chewy) caramel squares, unwrapped

CRUMBLE

⅔ cup all-purpose flour

½ cup light brown sugar

¼ cup white sugar

½ teaspoon ground cinnamon

1 pinch salt

¼ cup cold butter (½ stick)

1 SPRAY the crock of a slow cooker with non-stick cooking spray.

2 PLACE apples, cornstarch, first measure of sugar, lemon juice, water, and apple pie spice in the slow cooker and toss to thoroughly coat apples. Top apples with caramel squares.

3 USE a fork to combine all CRUMBLE ingredients, cutting the cold butter into the dry ingredients.

4 CRUMBLE the mixed topping over top of apples and caramels in slow cooker.

5 COVER, set cooker to HIGH, and let cook 2 hours.

6 TURN cooker off, uncover, and let stand 15 minutes before serving.

Helpful Hint

The caramels in this recipe are just like eating a caramel apple, but if you want something that will stick to your teeth less, try substituting soft butterscotch morsels/chips.

White Chocolate and Tangerine Rice Pudding

Rice Pudding Elevated to a Whole New Level

White chocolate and citrus, especially tangerines, go amazingly well together. The creaminess of the white chocolate cuts the acidity of the tangerine, leaving a more subtle and sweet flavor. It's no surprise then that these flavors go well in this homemade rice pudding recipe.

Shopping List

6 cups 2% (reduced-fat) milk

¾ cup long-grain white rice

¾ cup sugar

2 large eggs

¼ cup half-and-half

¾ teaspoon vanilla extract

1 pinch salt

1 cup white chocolate chips

Zest of 2 tangerines, finely chopped

Helpful Hint

If the pudding over-thickens, simply thin out with additional milk, just until it has reached your desired consistency.

1 PLACE milk, rice, and sugar in the crock of a slow cooker and stir to combine.

2 SET cooker to HIGH, cover, and let cook 30 minutes.

3 STIR, reduce cooker to LOW, cover, and let cook 5 additional hours.

4 IN a mixing bowl, thoroughly whisk eggs, half-and-half, vanilla extract, and salt. Continue whisking as you spoon in a large spoonful of the hot rice mixture. Once combined, whisk another spoonful of the hot rice mixture into the egg mixture. This will keep the eggs from curdling in the next step.

5 THOROUGHLY fold the egg mixture into the remaining rice mixture in the slow cooker. Then stir in white chocolate chips and tangerine zest.

6 SET cooker to HIGH, cover, and let cook 30 additional minutes, or until rice is tender and pudding has thickened. Stir every 15 minutes to prevent scorching as the pudding thickens.

7 SERVE warm or chilled.

Peach Crumble

With Toasted Almonds

A great summer dessert! Nothing pairs with peaches quite like toasted almonds—it's been scientifically proven! Peaches and almonds actually share so much of the same flavor compound that some almond extracts are made from peach pits.

Shopping List

PEACHES

32 ounces frozen peach slices

3 tablespoons cornstarch

¼ cup sugar

⅓ cup water

CRUMBLE

½ cup all-purpose flour

½ cup toasted almond slivers

½ cup light brown sugar

½ teaspoon ground cinnamon

1 pinch salt

¼ cup cold butter (½ stick)

1 SPRAY the crock of a slow cooker with non-stick cooking spray.

2 PLACE frozen peach slices in cooker, and then whisk together remaining PEACHES ingredients. Pour over top of peaches.

3 USE a fork to combine all CRUMBLE ingredients, cutting the cold butter into the dry ingredients.

4 CRUMBLE the mixed topping over top of peaches in slow cooker.

5 COVER, set cooker to HIGH, and let cook 2 hours.

6 TURN cooker off, uncover, and let stand 15 minutes before serving.

Helpful Hint

Toast slivered almonds in a large skillet over medium heat to toast. Shake the pan every 30 seconds to redistribute almonds, just until they are golden brown.

Bob Warden

about the author

Well-known TV personality **Bob Warden** has proven taste and sizzling passion for great food as a television cooking celebrity, kitchenware developer, and cookbook author. He is a hugely successful TV cooking show host, product developer, and QVC manufacturers' representative, with four decades of experience. Bob has helped develop more than 500 kitchen products for QVC, as well as for other top brand kitchen manufacturers. Bob has written nearly a dozen cookbooks including *Bob Warden's Slow Food Fast*, and *Bob Warden's Great Food Fast*. Warden's newest venture, Great Chefs International, includes the launch of a TV series, companion cookbook, and the premiere of **Great Flavors**, a new collection of low-sodium, high-taste concentrated stock bases.

about the photography

The food photographs in this book were taken by **Christian and Elise Stella**, under the guidance of Bob Warden. All food in the photographs was purchased at an ordinary grocery store and prepared exactly to the recipe's directions. This is exactly how the food should look in your own home. No artificial food styling techniques were used to "enhance" the food's appearance. Only water was sometimes spritzed on the food to keep it looking fresh during the thirty-minute photo shoots. No food prepared for photographs went to waste. All photographs were shot on a Canon 5dmkiii with a Zeiss 35mm f/2 lens.

Recipe Index

Beef

Poultry

Pork

Recipe Index (continued)